For my mother,
a splendid guiri *who would have gotten*
a kick out of this book.

SPANISH
AMONG AMIGOS

Conversational Spanish Beyond the Classroom

NURIA AGULLÓ

McGraw·Hill

New York   Chicago   San Francisco   Lisbon   London   Madrid   Mexico City
Milan   New Delhi   San Juan   Seoul   Singapore   Sydney   Toronto

Library of Congress Cataloging-in-Publication Data

Agulló, Nuria.
  Spanish among amigos : conversational Spanish beyond the classroom / Nuria Agulló.
    p.   cm.
  English and Spanish.
  ISBN 0-07-141514-9 (alk. paper)

  1. Spanish language—Conversation and phrase books—English. I. Title.

PC4121.A27 2003
468.3'421—dc21   2003056158

2 3 4 5 6 7 8 9 10 11   AGM/AGM   3 2 1 0 9 8 7 6 5 4

ISBN 0-07-141514-9

Interior design by Village Typographers, Inc.

McGraw-Hill books are available at special quantity discounts to use as premiums and sales promotions, or for use in corporate training programs. For more information, please write to the Director of Special Sales, Professional Publishing, McGraw-Hill, Two Penn Plaza, New York, NY 10121-2298. Or contact your local bookstore.

This book is printed on acid-free paper.

Contents

1
¡Me chiflas!

2
Nos llevamos de miedo

3
¡Qué petardo!

4
¡Es la monda!

5
Eres una fresca...

6
Pareces otra

Introduction

So you know some Spanish and can basically get by. Or so you thought till you started hanging out with native Spanish speakers. All of a sudden you're confronted with words and expressions you never saw in a textbook or phrasebook. What's worse, even the words you know you sometimes don't understand in context. And then you start to say something but get stuck because you don't know a really common everyday word.

Never fear! Pepa and Pili, our star duo live from Madrid, have come to the rescue! As you flip through these pages, these Spanish gals will make you smile, frown, chuckle, raise your eyebrows, and—most important of all—learn! And if you don't get what they're saying at first, don't worry: we'll make sure you do in the end. What's more, we'll give you lots of opportunities to jump in and fill in where necessary.

In short, *Spanish Among Amigos* is a hands-on vocabulary builder that presents informal everyday Spanish in context. But that doesn't mean we'll just be focusing on idioms and slang, which—let's face it—make up only about 5 percent of most everyday conversations. Rather, we'll be immersing you in dialogues that feel so natural and spontaneous you'll swear you're eavesdropping. And at the same time you'll pick up common words and expressions related to a broad range of topics. Along the way, we bet you'll also be entertained and gain a few insights into Spanish culture.

So who exactly are Pepa and Pili? And why the campy names? Are they meant to be cute? Well, yes and no. Actually, Pepa is a nickname for Maria José and Pili is short for Pilar, both common female names in Spain and Latin America (though the nickname "Pepa" is used only in Spain). The Pepa and Pili you'll be getting to know in this book are two sassy young women from Madrid. They also happen to be close friends, though they spend a lot of their time arguing, poking fun, and insulting each other.

Which brings us to lesson number one in informal Spanish. No, familiarity does not breed contempt, but it does give you a certain license. In fact (and this is particularly true in Spain), if people are too polite or try to spare one another's feelings, they'll probably be considered phony, weird, or even a little suspicious. Not that we're recommending that you let it all rip. As a foreigner, you have an excuse, and your Spanish-speaking friends will find your politeness and reticence charming. We just don't want you to get traumatized or offended if your amigo remarks that you've gained a little weight, or teases you for being a snob, wimp, or cheapskate. Take it in stride and smile if you can. It's a sign of affection and that you're part of the gang.

And now for a little confession. Yes, this book has a Spain slant, given that its main characters live in Madrid, as does its author. Having said this, we've tried to walk that fine line of being both local and universal. With this aim in mind, most of the vocabulary in this book is standard Spanish, common to most, if not all, Spanish-speaking countries. But since any true-to-life conversation has to have an authentic ring, you'll find some words and expressions here that are just used in Spain, including common colloquial terms.

Also, you'll find a few notes and remarks on some common aspects and features of Spain's culture. Where possible, we've also included comments on Latin America, but of course one author or one book can't pretend to cover all the cultural richness of the Spanish-speaking world. So we offer our apologies for being a little Spain-centric, and we hope that the comments about Spain and the Spanish can also serve as a springboard for discussion and comparison with other Spanish-speaking countries.

Now that you know what to expect, a round of thank-yous is in order. First I'd like to thank my editor at McGraw-Hill, Garret Lemoi, as well as Christopher Brown and Katherine Dennis for getting this *librito* into print.

A big thanks also to Pedro Garcia and Juan Larrea for their deft and razor-sharp editing, comments, and suggestions; Francesca Zucchetti for her invaluable input on Latin American usage; and Miguel Rosillo Fairén, whose sass and wit were a true source of inspiration.

Finally, a warm thanks to my friends and family for their help, support, and encouragement. I'd especially like to thank my sister, Jessica Agulló; my niece, Lotte Agulló-Collins; Trisha Ballsrud; Rocío Cassinello; Cristina Cid; Javier Fernández del Vallado; my father, José María García-Agulló; Antonio Gamboa; Enrique García; Luis Miguel González Cruz; Scott Goodell; Liz Mason; Declan Mulcahy; Donald Murphy; Beth Powers; Beatriz Pumarino; Oscar Temiño; and Anna María Villagarcía.

That's it. Dig in, enjoy, and learn!

How This Book Works

Spanish Among Amigos consists of twenty-one short units, each dealing with a specific subject, such as love, work, travel, money, shopping, vacations, and so on. We've arranged the units this way because vocabulary is absorbed more easily when it's presented in theme-related clusters. Also, since the point is to really immerse you in the language, there are no translations of the dialogues within the units and headings appear in Spanish.

   The units all have the same structure, which breaks down as follows:

Dialogue between Pepa and Pili

This dialogue opens the unit and presents the key vocabulary in context. The idea is for you to dive into the conversation and follow it as much as you can without the crutch of an accompanying English translation. (English versions of all of Pepa and Pili's dialogues appear at the end of the book, but we recommend you only refer to them later for consultation or if you're really confused or lost.)

¿Lo has captado? (Did you get it?)

This is a multiple-choice comprehension check (in English) to see if you understood Pepa and Pili's dialogue.

¡Al grano! (Let's get right to the point!)

This zeros in on the key vocabulary of the unit: words and expressions that are directly related to the theme, with English translations and/or equivalents. For easy reference, all *¡Al grano!* vocabulary appears in **bold** in Pepa and Pili's dialogue.

¡Ojo! (Note!)

This highlights vocabulary that is *not* directly related to the theme of the unit, but that you may not be familiar with. These extra words and expressions appear in ***bold italics*** in Pepa and Pili's dialogue.

Note that vocabulary is presented only once. That is, once a word or expression has appeared in an *¡Al grano!* or *¡Ojo!* section of a unit, it will not reappear in any of the subsequent units' lists (but of course it can always be found in the glossary at the end of the book). Since many words crop up again in subsequent units and the dialogues become a little meatier as the book progresses, we recommend that you read the units in the order in which they appear, although they can also be read in random order

Additional notes or commentary

After the vocabulary lists, there will often be a special note on a word or expression that appears in Pepa and Pili's dialogue. This could be a closer look at the word or expression in question, a list of similar expressions that are common in conversational Spanish, or useful additional vocabulary related to the theme of the unit.

¡Te toca! (Your turn!)

Here you'll begin to practice using the key vocabulary from the unit. This exercise might involve filling in the blanks, choosing the best word, matching synonyms, completing a dialogue, or responding to specific situations.

Intercambio (Language exchange)

Since you may not be familiar with this term, *intercambios* are informal conversation classes in which two people of different mother tongues meet regularly to help each other improve their language skills. (This, in fact, is very popular in Spain between Spaniards and speakers of other languages.) Each unit will close with an *intercambio* session between either Pepa or Pili and Tom, an American who has recently moved to Madrid. Your job is to jump in and complete the dialogue by filling in the blanks with key vocabulary from the unit. (This is a sink-or-swim exercise! The *intercambio* dialogues have no translations.)

Finally, you'll find the answer key to the exercises in each unit, English versions of Pepa and Pili's dialogues, and a Spanish-English glossary at the end of the book.

Abbreviations Used in This Book

Most of the vocabulary in this book is standard Spanish common to Latin America and Spain. Abbreviations (appearing in brackets) after a word or expression denote the following:

[col]   A colloquial word or expression used in most of Latin America and Spain, such as *un montón* for *a lot*.

[col, Spain] A colloquial word or expression used only in Spain, like *alucinante* for *incredible*.

[LA]   A Latin American equivalent of a word used only in Spain. For example, *manejar* would appear as the Latin American equivalent of *conducir*, meaning *to drive*.

[Spain]   A word or expression that is commonly used in Spain, but not elsewhere, such as *un piso* for *an apartment*.

[syn]   A synonym used in both Latin America and Spain. For example *una dieta* would appear as a synonym for *un régimen*, *a diet*, which is used only in Spain.

[var]   A common variation on a word. *Fuertote* is a variation of the adjective *fuerte*, or *strong*.

1

¡Me chiflas!

Pili's smitten again

Pili   Oye, Pepa, ¿sabes qué? Creo que **me he enamorado** otra vez.

Pepa   *¡No me digas!* ¿De ese chico que conociste la otra noche? ¿El **guaperas** ése?

Pili   Es **un encanto de persona.** De hecho, **estoy loca por él.**

Pepa   *¡Qué peligro!* A ver si vas a **perder la cabeza por** ese Don Juan.

Pili   Pues parece que yo **le gusto** bastante también. Hasta creo que **está un poco quedado conmigo.** Anoche me dijo que me **amaba** locamente.

Pepa   Eso lo dicen todos. Oye, Pili, ten mucho cuidado, que ya sabes que eres muy **enamoradiza.** Además, acabas de **romper** con Luis y no sería mala idea esperar un poco antes de tener otro **lío.**

Pili   Mira, Pepa, **te adoro,** pero eres una pesada. Ya sabes que a Luis **lo aprecio mucho,** pero nuestra **historia** no iba a *durar*. Pero, vamos a ver, el *tío* éste **me chifla.** Realmente **me cae genial.** De hecho, estoy convencida de que es el futuro padre de mis hijos.

Pepa   Bueno, *vale, tía*, pero espero que no le hayas dicho que lo **quieres** ni nada de eso.

Pili   Oye, *guapa*, romántica soy, ¡pero no *tonta perdida*! **Me encanta** este *tío*, pero sé mejor que nadie que a los hombres hay que seducirlos con muchas *artimañas*. Así que de momento, nada. *Disfruto*, que la vida es breve...

¿Lo has captado?

_____ 1. The guy Pili has fallen in love with is:
   a. a distant relative
   b. a hunk
   c. a male model

_____ 2. According to Pili, the guy is:
   a. a bit of a father figure
   b. a wonderful person
   c. an amateur magician

_____ 3. Pili thinks that he is:
   a. quite laid back about things
   b. not entirely trustworthy
   c. a little hooked on her

_____ 4. Pepa thinks that Pili is:
   a. someone who falls in love easily
   b. someone who rarely falls in love
   c. a femme fatale type

_____ 5. Pepa reminds Pili that she:
   a. is still going out with Luis
   b. has just broken up with Luis
   c. is in the process of breaking up with Luis

_____ 6. Pili claims that she is:
   a. still in love with Luis
   b. very fond of Luis
   c. really sick of Luis

_____ 7. When Pili says *me chifla*, she means the guy:
   a. alarms her a little
   b. annoys her
   c. delights her

_____ 8. Pili is going to:
   a. declare her love to the guy
   b. let him call the shots
   c. use all her wits to seduce him

Zooming in on like and love . . . Spanish, like Italian and French, is a Romance language, meaning it's derived from Latin. But maybe you don't know that it's also ideally suited to *romance* with a little "r". . . . And it doesn't end there. It's a great vehicle for conveying affection and nonromantic love too. So we thought we'd kick off by looking at the different ways of expressing *like* and *love* in Spanish, along with their various nuances and/or levels of intensity. Ready? Here's how to go about declaring love, like, delight, fondness, and passion.

¡Al grano!

Te adoro	I adore you (*as in English, this can express nonromantic love too; it can also be used lightly or ironically*)
Te amo	I love you (*very romantic and intense; generally reserved for long-term love partners*)
Te aprecio	I really like and value you (*conveys the idea of appreciation, respect, and fondness*)
Te quiero	I love you (*a catch-all term; can be used with everyone—love partners, family, close friends, pets, and so on*)
Me caes bien	I like you ([var] *Me caes genial* = *I really like you*)
Me chiflas [col, Spain]	informal version of *me encantas* (*old slang, but still common*)
Me encantas	I just love you (*basically means, I think you're really great; can be romantic or not. Note that encantar and chiflar are basically more exuberant versions of gustar and are often used to express love for things: Me encanta ir al cine. Me chiflan las películas de Almodóvar.*)
Me gustas	I like you (*This has sexual/romantic connotations when used in reference to people. But if you say Me gusta ese escritor—that is, you're referring to someone you don't know personally—gustar doesn't have romantic or sexual connotations. Here it means you like the way the writer writes, not him as a person.*)

Estoy enamorado/a de ti	I'm in love with you
Estoy loco/a por ti	I'm crazy about you
Estoy quedado/a contigo [col, Spain]	I'm hung up on you

More words and expressions

enamoradizo/a	someone that falls in love easily or often
enamorarse (de alguien)	to fall in love (with someone) (*estar enamorado/a* = *to be in love*)
un encanto de persona	a wonderful person
un guaperas [Spain]	a hunk, a good-looking suave guy (*generally negative*)
una historia [col, Spain]	a relationship or affair
un lío [col, Spain]	an affair or fling (*More generally,* un lío *is a messy or confusing situation.*)
perder la cabeza (por alguien)	to fall madly in love (with someone)
romper (con alguien)	to break up (with someone)

¡Ojo!

artimañas	wiles, cunning
disfrutar	to have a good time; to enjoy oneself (*disfrutar de/con algo* = *to enjoy something*)
durar	to last
¡No me digas!	No! You're joking!
¡Qué peligro! [col, Spain]	Uh oh! Oh dear!
perdido/a [col, Spain]	totally (*tonto perdido* = *totally stupid*)
un/a pesado/a	a bore or pain in the neck
un tío/una tía [col, Spain]	a guy/gal ([LA] *un tipo/una tipa.* *Note that* tío *and* tía *are also used informally in Spain to address friends and acquaintances;* guapo *and* guapa *are used much the same way, but have a little more punch.*)
Vale [col, Spain]	OK; all right

Get It Right!

¿«Amar» con o sin «a»?

Remember that **adorar**, **amar**, **apreciar**, and **querer** are *only* followed by the preposition **a** if the object of your affection, appreciation, or adoration is a person (or a much-loved pet). Note also that, without the preposition **a**, **querer** means *to want*.

Adoro *a* ese actor.	*versus*	Adoro el teatro.
Amo *a* María.	*versus*	Amo la vida.
A Luis lo aprecio mucho.	*versus*	Aprecio mucho tu interés.
Quiero mucho *a* mi madre.	*versus*	Quiero un café.

¡Te toca!

Complete the following sentences using one of the words or expressions below. (Use each word or phrase only once.)

me caen bien	adoro	me gustan	quiero
amo	me encanta	aprecio	estoy loco/a por

1. _____ viajar.

2. _____ mucho a mi gato.

3. _____ tus amigos.

4. _____ a mi hermano.

5. _____ los hombres morenos/las mujeres morenas.

6. _____ mi novio/a.

7. _____ mucho a mis amigos.

8. _____ a mi esposo/a.

Intercambio

Pili has recently begun an *intercambio* with Tom, an American who's just moved to Madrid. (See "How This Book Works" for an explanation of *intercambio*.) As you read their dialogue, fill in the blanks as Pili sets Tom straight and he corrects his gaffes. Tom's mistakes are underlined.

Tom   <u>Yo encanto a Marilyn Monroe.</u>

Pili   Pero ¡cómo vas a encantar a Marilyn Monroe! Para empezar, está muerta. Será que *ella te encanta*.

Tom   ¡Ah, sí! (1) _____ _____ Marilyn Monroe.

Pili   Eso es.

Tom   Gracias por tu ayuda, Pili. Eres muy paciente conmigo.

Pili   De nada, Tom. Es un placer.

Tom   De hecho, <u>yo te gusto</u> mucho, Pili.

Pili   Oye, guapo, me pareces simpático, ¡pero eso no significa que me gustes! A lo mejor es que yo te gusto...

Tom   ¡Ah sí!, perdón. Tú (2) _____ _____, Pili.

Pili   Lo siento mucho, Tom, pero yo te considero un amigo, nada más...

Tom   No me entiendes. Sólo quiero decir que eres un

           (3) _____ de persona.

Pili   ¡Ah, bueno! Entonces *te caigo bien*, no *te gusto*... ¡Menos mal!

Tom   Sí, (4) _____ _____ bien. Pero <u>soy enamorado</u> de otra.

Pili   Vaya... Pero no puedes *ser* enamorado de alguien. No es algo permanente.

Tom   Sí lo es. Mi amor por ella es para siempre.

Pili   Da igual. No forma parte de tu identidad. *Eres*, por ejemplo, americano y se ve que *eres* muy romántico, pero

           (5) _____ enamorado de esa chica. Por cierto, ¿quién es?

Tom   Tu amiga Pepa.

Pili   ¡Pepa! Pero no la conoces...

Tom   No importa. La he visto por la calle contigo. Escucha, Pili,

           (6) _____ _____ por ella.

Pili   ¡Vaya por Dios! Pues nada, ya te la presentaré...

2

Nos llevamos de miedo

Pepa and Pili chat about relationships

Pepa   Así que **sigues con** ese *pibe*, Pili.

Pili   Pues sí, y nos está yendo bastante bien. *Fíjate*, ya **llevamos tres meses juntos**.

Pepa   Es verdad. Me acuerdo de que te lo **ligaste** en Semana Santa y ya estamos en julio. ¡Increíble!

Pili   La verdad es que sí. Y **nos llevamos** *de miedo*. Además, parece que **la relación va en serio**.

Pepa   Y yo que pensé que no ibais a durar, que era **una aventura de primavera**...

Pili   *De eso nada*. Por fin **me he echado un novio** de verdad. De hecho, sigo convencida de que es el hombre de mi vida.

Pepa   *¡Qué suerte!*, Pili. A ver si llego a **conocer a** alguien así un día de estos.

Pili   Pues *ya es hora*. *Dejaste de* **salir con** Javi hace un año y desde entonces no **te has enrollado** con nadie. Ni siquiera un **ligue** para *levantarte la moral*

Pepa   Mira, Pili, ya sabes que esas cosas **no me van**. Ni **los sitios de ligar** tampoco. Prefiero encontrarme un tío de una forma *sana* y natural. A través de amigos, en *un cursillo*, en el trabajo...

Pili   Oye, ¿y el americano que te **presenté** el otro día? ¿**Qué tal te cayó**?

Pepa   Ah, muy bien, pero no creo que sea mi **tipo**. De todas formas, me pidió el teléfono y vamos a **quedar** un día de estos...

¿Lo has captado?

_____ 1. Three months down the line, things between Pili and her boyfriend are:
    a. still good
    b. getting a little lukewarm
    c. getting a bit too serious

_____ 2. Pili and her boyfriend:
    a. are planning to get engaged
    b. get a little scared at times
    c. get along really well

_____ 3. Pepa would like to:
    a. meet someone
    b. go out more
    c. take a night course

_____ 4. Since Pepa broke up with Javi, she:
    a. hasn't even had a fling
    b. hasn't gotten involved with anyone
    c. both _a_ and _b_

_____ 5. Pepa doesn't like meeting men:
    a. at bars
    b. in chat rooms
    c. through dating agencies

_____ 6. Pepa thinks the guy Pili introduced her to the other day is:
    a. a bit of a wimp
    b. not very attractive
    c. quite nice

_____ 7. Pepa and the American guy have agreed to:
    a. get together soon
    b. call each other
    c. stay in touch

Zooming in on relationships and romance... We dealt with liking and loving in the last unit. We're now going to go beyond the realm of sentiment and into the "real" world of introductions, meetings, relationships, and romance. And while we're on this topic, how could we not include a special note on two verbs that have become part of the general lexicon in Spain? You got it—the indispensable *quedar* and *ligar*. . . .

¡Al grano!

una aventura	an affair
conocer a alguien	to meet someone (for the first time)
echarse un/a novio/a [col, Spain]	to get oneself a boyfriend/girlfriend
enrollarse (con alguien) [col, Spain]	to get involved (with someone)
ligar (a alguien) [col, Spain]	to pick up (someone), to score (*See "Getting Together" later in this unit.*)
un ligue [col, Spain]	a casual fling or relationship
llevar (un año) juntos	to have been together (for a year)
llevarse bien	to get along well ([var] *llevarse de miedo* = *to get along great or "scarily" well*)
No me va [col, Spain]	It isn't for me; It's not my style
un/a novio/a	a boyfriend/girlfriend (*this can also mean fiancé/fiancée*)
presentar a alguien	to introduce someone [to somebody]
quedar (con alguien) [Spain]	to plan or arrange to get together (with someone) (*See "Getting Together" later in this unit.*)
¿Qué tal te cayó?	What did you think of him/her? Did you like him/her? (*from caer bien/mal*)
una relación	a relationship
salir (con alguien)	to go out (with someone)
seguir (con alguien)	to be still seeing/going out (with someone)
sitios/bares de ligar [col, Spain]	singles' bars
tipo	type
Va en serio	It's for real; It's serious

¡Ojo!

un cursillo [Spain]	a short course
De eso nada	No way! Are you kidding!
dejar de (salir, hacer, etc.)	to stop (going out with, doing, etc.)
de miedo [col, Spain]	great, fantastic(ally)
Fíjate	Just think! Get this!
levantar la moral	to raise one's spirits
un pibe/una piba	a boy/girl (very common in Argentina; is used by some young people in Spain)
¡Qué suerte!	Lucky you!
sano/a	healthy, wholesome
Ya es hora	It's about time

Getting Together

«Quedar» y «ligar»

These two seemingly harmless verbs can really throw you off if you don't know their colloquial meanings. Since they crop up all the time in informal (and not so informal) conversations in Spain, we're going to take a closer look at them here.

Quedar [col, Spain] This word roughly means *to have a plan to meet up with someone*. So *He quedado con Paco mañana* would translate as *I'm seeing (or meeting up with) Paco tomorrow*. Meanwhile, let's say a friend asks you if you want to meet up later and you've already made other plans. In this case, you'd reply *No puedo, he quedado* (*I can't, I've made other plans* or *I can't, I'm busy*). This expression has a very opaque and final element, so it can also come in handy when you don't want to give explanations or go into details.

Ligar [col, Spain] This verb doesn't even have a rough English equivalent, though it's sometimes loosely translated as *to score* or *to pick up (someone)*. Basically, it's a totally ambiguous word that covers anything resulting from two people meeting and feeling physically attracted to each other. *He ligado* could just mean *I flirted with* or *exchanged phone numbers with someone*, though it could also mean you ended up in wild abandon together. Note, though, that *un ligue* doesn't have this ambiguity and is clearly either *a casual relationship* or *a person with whom one's having a casual relationship*.

¡Te toca!

A week later Pepa and Pili meet up for coffee. Complete their dialogue by underlining the word that fits best.

Pili   ¿Qué sabes de Tom? ¿Te llamó?

Pepa   Sí, (1) **quedamos** | **ligamos** | **llevamos** para ir al cine la semana pasada, y todo muy bien... En fin, gracias por habérmelo (2) **introducido** | **conocido** | **presentado**.

Pili   ¿Ah, sí? Cuéntame. ¿Estás (3) **viendo** | **saliendo** | **ligando** con él ahora?

Pepa   Sí, y la verdad es que nos (4) **llevamos** | **salimos** | **seguimos** muy bien.

Pili   ¡Cuánto me alegro! ¡Y eso que me dijiste que no era tu (5) **ligue** | **tipo** | **tío**.

Pepa   Pues nada, chica. Creo que por fin me he echado un (6) **amigo** | **pibe** | **novio**.

Intercambio

Several days later, Pili and Tom meet up for their *intercambio*. Fill in the blanks as you read their dialogue.

Tom   Gracias por <u>introducirme</u> a Pepa.

Pili   De nada. Pero no te la *introduje*, Tom, te la (1) _____.

Tom   Ah sí, es verdad.

Pili   Bueno, ¿qué tal? ¿Quedaste con ella?

Tom   No, después del cine me fui a casa.

Pili   Entonces sí *quedaste* con ella, os fuisteis al cine...

Tom   Ah sí, perdona. (2) _____ con ella el lunes. Fuimos a ver una película de <u>una aventura</u>.

Pili   ¡Qué bonito! La llevaste a una película romántica...

Tom   Romántica no. Era una película de Schwarzenegger.

Pili   ¡Ah!, una película de *acción*. Es que una (3) _____ es
          una historia de amor, sabes...

Tom   ¡Ajá!, como lo que tengo con Pepa...

Pili   Si es algo que no va a durar, entonces sí. Normalmente se trata
          de un amor pasional e imposible.

Tom   ¡Ah no! Esto va a durar. Pepa y yo vamos en (4) _____.

Pili   Pues entonces tienes una (5) _____ con ella, no una
          aventura.

Tom   Sí, claro, Pepa es mi <u>amiga</u>.

Pili   Bueno, pero yo también soy tu *amiga*, Tom. Más que amiga,

          Pepa es tu (6) _____.

3

¡Qué petardo!

Pepa and Pili try to avoid someone they can't stand

Pili No mires, Pepa, pero acaba de entrar el tío más **odioso** del planeta...

Pepa ¡Ah!, ya sé quién dices, ése de la camisa naranja. Tienes toda la razón, es **un pesado**. Yo **tampoco lo aguanto**.

Pili ¡No lo mires! Si se acerca a nuestra mesa, **me voy a poner mala**. De verdad, a ese tío **no lo soporto**.

Pepa A mí también **me cae fatal**. Además, es un **cotilla** *de mucho cuidado*. Es de los que **ponen a parir** a la gente **a sus espaldas**.

Pili *¿Ah sí?* Pues eso es otra cosa que **me saca de quicio**. Pero, ¡si **no hay quien aguante** a ese **petardo**! Y encima es un arrogante.

Pepa Es verdad, Pili, es un ser totalmente **repugnante**. Y su sonrisa no me gusta nada tampoco. Es más falsa que el color de tu pelo.

Pili Oye, guapa, **no te metas con** mi nuevo "look", que me ha costado *un ojo de la cara*.

Pepa *Tranquila*, sólo *era un decir*. *Anda*, termina tu cerveza rápido, que vamos a escaparnos antes de que nos vea ese **imbécil**.

Pili Ya nos ha visto. ¡Se nos está acercando! ¡Dios mío, Pepa, **me voy a poner enferma** de verdad! *Venga*, paga al camarero y vámonos *corriendo*...

¿Lo has captado?

_____ 1. Pepa and Pili are chatting over:
   a. a beer
   b. lunch
   c. coffee

_____ 2. Pepa and Pili both think that the guy in the orange shirt is:
   a. a jerk
   b. really tacky
   c. mentally ill

_____ 3. Pili says that if he approaches their table, she will:
   a. pass out
   b. give him a dirty look
   c. get sick

_____ 4. Pepa and Pili also don't like the fact that the guy is:
   a. a gossip
   b. a leech
   c. a two-timer

_____ 5. Neither Pepa nor Pili like people who are:
   a. stingy
   b. two-faced
   c. pseudo-intellectual

_____ 6. Pepa thinks the guy's smile is:
   a. tight-lipped
   b. phony
   c. lewd

_____ 7. At the end, Pili says **Dios mío** because the guy is:
   a. walking towards them
   b. waving at them
   c. leering at them

Zooming in on dislike and irritation . . . We've looked at how to go about expressing like and love. But what if someone or something really grates on your nerves? Not to worry. You also have loads of options for expressing dislike, irritation, and loathing. The following is a list of some of the most common ones.

¡Al grano!

detesto	I hate (*very strong*)
me cae mal/fatal	I dislike/I really dislike him/her (*only for people*)
me horroriza	I hate, I can't stand
me irrita	he/she/it annoys or irritates me
me pone enfermo/a [Spain]	he/she/it makes me ill ([LA] *me enferma*)
me pone malo/a [Spain]	he/she/it makes me sick ([LA] *me enferma*)
me saca de quicio	he/she/it really gets on my nerves or drives me up the wall
no aguanto	I can't bear, I can't stand ([var] *No hay quién lo aguante* = *Who can put up with him/her/it?*)
no me cae bien	I don't like (*only for people*)
no me gusta (nada)	I don't like (at all)
no soporto	I can't take, I can't stand
odio	I hate (*very strong*)

More words and expressions

a sus espaldas	behind his/her/their back
un/a cotilla [Spain]	a gossip ([syn] *un/a chismoso/a*)
falso/a	fake, phony
un/a imbécil	an idiot or jerk (*See "Poking Fun and Insulting" later in this unit.*)
inaguantable	unbearable
insoportable	intolerable, very tedious or annoying
meterse con (algo/alguien)	to verbally attack or criticize (something/someone)
odioso/a	loathsome; despicable
(un/a) pesado/a (*adj and n*)	a pain in the neck, a bore (*See "Poking Fun and Insulting" later in this unit.*)
(un/a) petardo/a [col, Spain] (*adj and n*)	a jerk, a bore (*See "Poking Fun and Insulting" later in this unit.*)
poner a parir (a alguien) [col, Spain]	to diss or speak badly of (someone)
repugnante	horrible, disgusting

¡Ojo!

¿Ah sí?	Oh yeah? Really?
Anda	Come on
corriendo	right away, immediately
de mucho cuidado	big, real, terrible (*un cotilla de mucho cuidado* = *a real gossip*)
Era un decir	Don't take it the wrong way (*literally, It was just a saying*)
un ojo de la cara	an arm and a leg, a fortune
Tranquilo/a	Calm down; Don't worry
Venga [col, Spain]	Come on

Poking Fun and Insulting

¡Es un pesado!

Want to poke fun at, insult, or rant about somebody? Here are some ways to go about it. We've classified these common invectives into three groups of synonyms and provided the masculine form here. (For the feminine form, simply use the female article, end the noun in *a*—unless it already ends in *a*, like *idiota*, *pelma*, and *plasta*—and you're in business.) Finally, note that most of these terms can also be used teasingly and even affectionately among friends.

Bastards and sons of bitches

un cabrón	*vulgar and very strong*
un cerdo	*a more standard alternative; this can also mean* a pig *or* slob
un hijo de puta	*very vulgar and very strong*

Idiots, jerks, and assholes

un bobo	*a tamer alternative*
un gilipollas [Spain]	*vulgar and very strong*
un idiota	*very common*
un imbécil	*very common; has more punch than* bobo, idiota, *or* tonto
un payaso	*literally, a clown but can also mean* an idiot

| un tonto | quite tame |
| un tonto del culo [col, Spain] | stronger, more vulgar variation of *un tonto* |

Major bores and pains in the neck/ass

un pelma [Spain]	someone who goes on and on or just won't leave you alone
un pesado	the most common and general term
un petardo [col, Spain]	this can also mean *a jerk*
un plasta [col, Spain]	very common; used in much the same way as *pelma*

¡Te toca!

Complete the sentences using one of the words or expressions from below.

| no soporto | poner a parir | odio | no me gustan nada |
| una pesada | le cae muy mal | un imbécil | me saca de quicio |

1. _____ a los niños maleducados.

2. A Pepe _____ el novio de María.

3. _____ a la gente hipócrita.

4. _____ las películas violentas.

5. Esa mujer es realmente _____.

6. Ese tío es _____.

7. A Boris le encanta _____ a los demás.

8. Esperar es una cosa que _____.

Intercambio

Tom's been having problems with his boss and decides to unload on Pili when they meet for their *intercambio*. Fill in the blanks as you read their dialogue.

Pili   ¿Qué tal?, Tom.

Tom   Pues mal. No me llevo bien con mi jefe.

Pili   ¿Qué pasa? ¿No le caes bien?

Tom   No lo sé, pero se (1) _____
conmigo todo el tiempo. Es un gran dolor.

Pili   Creo que quieres decir que es *un pesado*.

Tom   Sí. Y después me critica detrás de mi espalda.

Pili   La expresión correcta es (2) _____ _____ _____.
Pues entonces es un hombre un poco repugnante...

Tom   Sí, es totalmente odioso. En fin, (3) _____ _____ fatal.

Pili   No me sorprende. Anda, relájate y olvídate de ese petardo.

Tom   No puedo. Es que realmente me saca (4) _____

_____.

Pili   Claro, es un imbécil. A mí también me pondría (5) _____.

Tom   Y encima es un hipócrita. En fin, no soporto a él.

Pili   Puedes decir *no soporto a mi jefe*, pero no puedes decir *no soporto a él*.

Tom   ¡Ah!, se dice (6) _____ _____ _____.

Pili   Así es. Bueno, me parece que no vas a durar mucho más en tu trabajo.

Tom   No, porque es una situación realmente (7) _____.

4

¡Es la monda!

Pepa and Pili don't see eye to eye

Pepa   ¿**Qué te pareció** la película?

Pili   **Horrorosa. Deprimente** *a tope*. Y ese tío, *el protagonista*, era realmente **repelente**... ¡**Qué asco**, de verdad!

Pepa   Pues a mí **me pareció** un actor **estupendo**, y la película un poco **tremenda**, pero muy bien hecha. ¿De verdad **te pareció** tan mala?

Pili   ¡Ay, por favor! ¡**Qué espanto, qué horror** *de* película! Prométeme que no me volverás a hacer esto.

Pepa   Pero fue tu idea ir a verla. Además, *las críticas* la ponían **fenomenal** y el actor ése es **bestial**... Eso sí, *el argumento* era un poco **fuerte**...

Pili   Mira, lo único que estuvo bien fue la primera novia del protagonista, *¡qué* actriz *más* **genial**!, y claro, ese tío tan *sumamente* **desagradable** la mata casi en seguida.

Pepa   Bueno, la próxima vez una comedia. Podríamos ver la última *peli* de Almodóvar, que dicen que es **divertidísima**.

Pili   ¡Pero si Almodóvar es **insoportable**! Me han gustado dos o tres películas suyas, las demás me parecen **pesadísimas**. Venga, está **pasado de moda** y *de* original y **gracioso** ya *no tiene nada*.

Pepa   Pues a mí **me encantó** su última película. **Me emocionó** de verdad.

Pili   *Vaya*. Para mí lo único **emocionante** de esa película fueron *los títulos de crédito* al final. Mira, tía, *paso de* Almodóvar, pero sí que iría a ver la de Woody Allen. Dicen que **es la monda**.

Pepa   *Venga, va*.

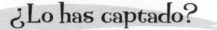

¿Lo has captado?

_____ 1. The movie that Pepa and Pili have just seen was probably:
   a. a sci-fi movie
   b. a thriller about a serial killer
   c. a western

_____ 2. The movie had received:
   a. OK reviews
   b. mixed reviews
   c. rave reviews

_____ 3. Pili thought the protagonist:
   a. was a terrible actor
   b. had a repulsive face
   c. was a slimy, disagreeable character

_____ 4. Pepa liked the movie, but agreed that it:
   a. was pretty disturbing
   b. overdid it on the sex scenes
   c. had a weak cast

_____ 5. According to the critics, Almodóvar's latest film is:
   a. his best yet
   b. a lot of fun
   c. very sardonic and worldly

_____ 6. Pili thinks most of Almodóvar's films are:
   a. funny and original
   b. tedious and repetitive
   c. boring and outdated

_____ 7. Pepa and Pili will probably:
   a. never go to the movies together again
   b. go see the latest Woody Allen movie
   c. never agree on any movie

Zooming in on stating opinions . . . Ask a Spanish friend his or her opinion of a movie or a book, and you'll probably get a pretty effusive response: *¡Buenísimo! ¡Qué maravilla! ¡Me espantó! ¡Horroroso!* Though formal and literary Spanish can be charged with subtlety and nuance, in everyday Spanish things tend to swing to both ends of the positive-negative spectrum. In fact, there's not much middle ground, so you may as well forget about sitting on the fence and just go with your gut reaction. Below you'll find some adjectives and expressions commonly used for giving opinions.

¡Al grano!

Common adjectives

POSITIVE

alucinante [col, Spain] amazing, incredible
bestial [col] fantastic, great
divertido/a fun, entertaining
emocionante exciting
estupendo/a fantastic
fabuloso/a fabulous
fenomenal [col, Spain] great
genial [col] great, wonderful
gracioso/a funny, amusing
increíble unbelievable, wild
magnífico/a great, magnificent
maravilloso/a great, wonderful
original inventive, original

NEGATIVE

cursi corny, prissy
deprimente depressing, a downer
desagradable nasty, unpleasant
espantoso/a dreadful, horrible
fuerte [col] shocking, disturbing
horrible terrible, horrible
horroroso/a awful, dreadful, hideous
insoportable very tedious or annoying
pasado/a de moda outdated, passé
pesado/a boring, tedious, longwinded
repelente disgusting, repulsive
tremendo/a [col, Spain] outrageous, extreme
violento/a violent

Common expressions

De (gracioso/a) no tiene nada	He/She/It's not (funny) at all.
Es la monda [col, Spain]	It's a real blast; it's really funny
¡Me encantó!	Loved it!
¡Me emocionó!	I really loved it! (*This can also mean "it was really moving" or "it hit the spot"*)
¡Me espantó! *or* **¡Me horrorizó!**	Horrible! I hated it!
Paso de (algo/alguien) [col, Spain]	I have no interest in (someone/something)
¿Qué te pareció (la película)?	What did you think of (the movie)?

¡Qué asco!	Gross! How disgusting!
¡Qué horror! *or* ¡Qué espanto!	Horrible! How dreadful!
¡Qué maravilla!	How wonderful! It was amazing!

(These exclamations beginning with *qué* can also be followed by *de* + a noun. For example, *¡Qué asco de película!* = *What a disgusting movie!* *¡Qué maravilla de libro!* = *What a great book!* Another common variation is explained in "Hearty Opinions" below.)

¡Ojo!

el argumento	the plot
a tope [col, Spain]	totally (*deprimente a tope* = *depressing to the max*)
una crítica	a review
una peli [col, Spain]	a movie (*abbreviated form of* **película**)
el/la protagonista	the hero/heroine, the main character
sumamente	totally, completely
los títulos de crédito [Spain]	the (film) credits ([LA] *los créditos*)
Vaya	Ah-ha; Oh dear
Venga, va [col, Spain]	OK, you're on

Hearty Opinions

¡Qué película más horrorosa!

This is an extremely common construction in Spanish. In fact, it's used quite a bit more than its English equivalent, *What a/an + adjective + noun!* (in this case, *"What an awful movie!"*). Note that the basic formula here is *¡Qué + noun + más + adjective!* And remember, the adjective always agrees with the noun.

¡Qué película más buena!	What a great movie!
¡Qué tío más cursi!	What a corny guy!
¡Qué libro más espantoso!	What a dreadful book!
¡Qué actriz más genial!	What a wonderful actress!

Needless to say, as in English, the variations are endless.

¡Te toca!

Underline the one word that *doesn't* work in the following sentences.

1. Me reí mucho con esa película. Era muy **divertida** | **genial** | **graciosa**.

2. No me gustan nada las películas violentas. Me parecen muy **desagradables** | **deprimentes** | **bestiales**.

3. El libro trata de una mujer que es drogadicta. En fin, tiene un argumento un poco **fuerte** | **tremendo** | **pesado**.

4. —¿Te gustó la peli?

   —Sí, me **espantó** | **encantó** | **emocionó**.

5. ¡Qué **horror** | **espanto** | **maravilla**! Los documentales sobre la guerra me deprimen mucho.

6. Te recomiendo esa película. Y el actor es **bestial** | **estupendo** | **espantoso**.

7. El protagonista del libro es un verdadero cerdo. Un hombre realmente **horrible** | **original** | **desagradable**.

8. ¡Qué actriz más **genial** | **maravillosa** | **fuerte**! De hecho, ganó el Oscar el año pasado.

The -ísimo quiz

Which of the following adjectives could you add the suffix *-ísimo* to if you wanted to give them extra force or stress? (Sorry, no *intercambio* in this unit, as Pili is *enamoradísima* and has canceled her session with Tom to go see her man.) See if your instincts and common sense can guide you on this.

1. bueno/a   _____

2. genial   _____   ¿**Maravillosísimo**?

3. pesado/a   _____

4. malo/a   _____

5. maravilloso/a   _____

6. bestial   _____

7. divertido/a   _____

8. gracioso/a   _____

Eres una fresca...

Pepa and Pili shiver and sweat

Pili ¡Qué **frío** hace aquí!, Pepa. ¡**Me estoy congelando**!

Pepa *¡Qué dices!* Fuera **hace un calor que te mueres**. *Menos mal* que hemos encontrado este refugio. Este aire **fresquito** es una delicia.

Pili Qué siberiana eres, chica. ¡Pero si parece que estamos en el Polo Norte! Eres **una calurosa** tremenda.

Pepa Y tú **una friolera** y una pesada.

Pili Pues la verdad es que a mí **el calorcito** del verano me encanta. Mira, o quitan el aire acondicionado o voy a *pillar* **un resfriado** *brutal*.

Pepa *¡Venga ya!* Tómate la sopa, que se te va a **enfriar**.

Pili Ya **está fría**. Es *gazpacho*, tía.

Pepa Pues que te lo **calienten**, *pelma*.

Pili *¡Ya está bien!*, Pepa, que de verdad **tengo mucho frío**. Tócame la mano y verás.

Pepa Tienes razón, Pili, **estás helada**. Venga, déjate el gazpacho y pide *un caldo*, y que te lo traigan **ardiendo**.

Pili Buena idea, aunque dudo que **esté tan caliente** como el camarero, que no para de mirarme. Le voy a sonreír y enseñar un poco de pierna, a ver cómo reacciona...

Pepa Eres **una fresca**, tía. *Para ya*, que lo vas a **calentar** al pobre.

Pili Pues vámonos de aquí, Pepa, que *no puedo más con* estas temperaturas glaciales. Anda, pide la cuenta y vamos a buscar *una terraza* al sol.

¿Lo has captado?

_____ 1. Pepa and Pili are in:
   a. a self-service cafeteria
   b. a restaurant
   c. a mountain refuge

_____ 2. When Pili says that Pepa is a *calurosa*, she means that she:
   a. has a bad case of heat stroke
   b. is hot-tempered
   c. is warm-blooded and would probably not mind living
      in Siberia

_____ 3. Pili says that if the air conditioning isn't turned off, she will:
   a. get a cold
   b. get a severe attack of the shivers
   c. go pale and pass out

_____ 4. Pili's hands are:
   a. cool
   b. icy cold
   c. warm

_____ 5. Pili thinks that the waiter:
   a. feels hot
   b. is very sexy
   c. is attracted to her

_____ 6. At the end, Pepa accuses Pili of:
   a. whining
   b. being provocative
   c. playing cool

_____ 7. Pili suggests going to:
   a. an outdoor café
   b. the terrace of her house
   c. a slab of stone where they can lie in the sun

Zooming in on hot and cold . . . As you probably know, Spanish is a little trickier than English when it comes to talking about the weather and just generally expressing notions of hot and cold. So though we don't want to go into grammar in this book, we're going to make a little exception here. Below is a brief breakdown to enlighten the clueless, which can also serve as a quick refresher for those of you who are a bit rusty or unsure.

¡Al grano!

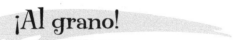

To the touch

Use **estar** + *an adjective* if you're talking about something that's hot or cold *to the touch* (objects, people, food, drink, and so on). So *This soup is very hot* would be **Esta sopa** *está* **muy caliente.** Remember the adjective (or complement) has to agree with the noun, so *This soup is cold* would be **Esta sopa está** *fría.* But if you say that a person *está caliente*, make sure the context is clear. It could of course mean they "feel" hot to you (they have a fever), but it could also mean they're horny or sexually "heated up."

Inner feeling

Use **tener** + *a noun* if you're talking about an *inner feeling* of hot or cold, just like you would if you were talking about being hungry or thirsty. Therefore *I'm hot* would be **Tengo calor**, just like *I'm hungry* is **Tengo hambre.** And since you're using a noun and not an adjective here, *I'm very hot* would be **Tengo** *mucho* **calor.**

The weather

Use **hacer** in the third person singular + *a noun* if you're talking about the weather. So *It's cold* would be **Hace frío** and *It's hot,* **Hace calor.** Likewise, *It's sunny* would be **Hace sol** and *It's windy,* **Hace viento.** Again, since you're using a noun, *It's very hot* would be **Hace** *mucho* **calor.**

Exclamations!

Finally, use **qué** + *the inverted form* of the appropriate structure to make an exclamation. So *Boy it's hot!* would be ¡**Qué calor** *hace!*, *I'm so hot!* would be ¡**Qué calor** *tengo!*, and *(The soup) is so hot!* would be ¡**Qué caliente** *está!* Note also the structure of ¡**Hace** *un* **calor** *que te mueres!* (*literally, It's so hot that you die!*)

Other words and expressions

al sol	in the sun
ardiendo	very hot, boiling (*from **arder**, which means to burn or to blaze*)
un caldo	a clear hot soup (*a broth or consommé*)
calentar	to heat up (*when applied to a person, it can mean "to turn on"*)
calorcito	pleasant warmth or heat (*See "Injecting a Little Emotion" later in this unit.*)
caluroso/a*	warm-blooded (*someone who often feels hot*)
congelarse	to freeze
enfriar	to get cold, to cool down
fresquito	chilly, cool (*diminutive of **fresco***)
fresco/a*	brazen or cheeky
friolero/a* [Spain]	cold-blooded (*someone who often feels cold;* [LA] ***friolento/a***)
gazpacho	a cold tomato-based soup (*a typical summer dish in Spain*)
helado/a	frozen (***helado** as a noun is ice cream*)
un resfriado	a cold

¡Ojo!

brutal [col, Spain]	tremendous, colossal
Menos mal	Thank God
¡Para ya! [Spain]	Stop it!
No puedo más con...	I can't take . . . ; I can't deal with . . .
un/a pelma [col, Spain]	a bore or pain in the neck (*See "Poking Fun and Insulting" in Unit 3.*)
pillar [col]	to catch, to get
¡Qué dices! [Spain]	Are you kidding!
una terraza [Spain]	an outdoor café
Venga ya [col, Spain]	Come on! Oh please!
¡Ya está bien!	That's enough!

*These adjectives can also be used as nouns for added emphasis.

Injecting a Little Emotion

Calor, calorcito, calorazo

As you know, suffixes often indicate size. But they also often express your feeling about something.

Take, for example, the diminutive suffix **-ito**. If you tack this onto a noun, it can indicate smallness, but it's also commonly used to express affection or pleasure. **Calorcito**, for instance, is not *little heat* but rather *pleasant heat*, and **Hace calorcito** means *It's nice and warm* or even *It's nice and hot*. You might say this, for example, if it's seventy-five degrees outside and you're basking in the sun or it's winter and you've just come into a toasty apartment.

Meanwhile, the suffix **-azo** cranks up the noun to a higher pitch and generally indicates largeness or greatness. But, depending on the noun you're using, this could convey awe or admiration (**un cochazo** is *a really great car*) or else displeasure and a sense of being overwhelmed. **Calorazo**, for example, would be *great* or *stifling heat* and you might hear someone exclaim ¡**Qué calorazo!** if the heat's on too high or it's over ninety degrees in the shade.

¡Te toca!

Fill in the blanks in the sentences below.

1. Soy muy friolero. Casi siempre _____ _____ frío.

2. El agua de la piscina _____ _____ muy fría.

3. ¡Qué _____ tengo! Me voy a dar una ducha fría.

4. Siempre _____ _____ en el desierto.

5. ¡_____ _____ hace! ¡Estoy helado!

6. Estás muy _____. ¿Tienes fiebre?

7. Llévate una chaqueta. _____ fresquito fuera.

8. Como soy _____, siempre duermo con la ventana abierta.

Intercambio

This week's *intercambio* has been canceled again, as Pili's come down with a nasty cold. Meanwhile, Pepa and Tom decide to get a little dose of culture and go to the Prado. But it's a hot summer day and the air-conditioning at the museum isn't working. . . .

Tom <u>Estoy muy caliente</u>, Pepa. No puedo más...

Pepa ¡Qué dices! ¿Te ha excitado "La Maja Desnuda"?

Tom ¡No me entiendes! ¡Este museo es como una sauna! ¡Es insoportable!

Pepa ¡Ah!, (1) _____ _____. Es que *estar caliente* es otra cosa, sabes...

Tom Ya veo. Pues (2) _____ mucho calor, Pepa. Realmente <u>es muy caliente</u> aquí.

Pepa No, Tom. Cuando hablas de la temperatura ambiental se usa el verbo *hacer*.

Tom Ah sí, es verdad. Pues (3) _____ _____

_____.

Pepa Sí, estamos en agosto y no tienen puesto el aire acondicionado. Los del museo son unos frescos...

Tom Sí, y tu amiga Pili es una (4) _____ también.

Pepa ¿Por qué? ¿Lo dices porque ha cancelado vuestro intercambio?

Tom Sí, es la segunda vez. Esta vez su excusa era que <u>tenía un frío</u>.

Pepa Bueno, Pili es muy friolera. Siempre (5) _____

_____. Pero dudo mucho que ésa fuese su excusa. Será que

tiene un (6) _____.

Tom ¡Ajá! En fin... "La Maja Desnuda" es realmente un cuadro fantástico.

Pepa Pues fue un escándalo cuando Goya lo pintó. Creo que él y la duquesa tuvieron una aventura muy pasional.

Tom Entonces Goya estaba (7) _____ cuando la pintó...

Pepa ¡Ahora lo has dicho bien! Oye, Tom, ¿nos vamos a tomar un helado? Hay una heladería buenísima cerca de aquí...

6

Pareces otra

Pepa's dolled up for her date

Pili   ¡Qué **guapa** estás, Pepa! **Pareces otra.**

Pepa   *¿Qué pasa?* ¿**Me ves** tan **horrorosa** normalmente?

Pili   Que no, tonta. Ya sabes que eres atractiva y **tienes buen tipo.** Pero hoy estás especialmente radiante. Además, esa chaqueta **te queda muy bien.**

Pepa   Me la compré el otro día en *las rebajas.* Es **bonita**, ¿verdad?

Pili   Sí, muy **mona.** Y ese color **te favorece** mucho.

Pepa   ¿Ah sí? Es un poco **llamativo**, pero bueno... *Por cierto*, ese bolsito que llevas es **una monada.** ¿Dónde lo compraste?

Pili   En una tienda muy **chula** en la calle Fuencarral. Tiene unas cosas *super* **graciosas** y originales. Pero cuéntame, Pepa, ¿por qué vas tan **arreglada** hoy? ¿Has quedado con Tom luego?

Pepa   Pues sí. Vamos a cenar en *un marroquí* que dicen que es muy bueno. Y creo que el sitio es un poco elegante.

Pili   ¿No será uno que está en la calle Recoletos?

Pepa   ¿Cómo lo sabías?

Pili   Porque es el único así. Bueno, Pepa, el sitio es **ideal**, ya verás. Y aparte de la decoración que es **preciosa**, los camareros son **guapísimos.** *¡Qué envidia!*, chica. *Te lo vas a pasar bomba.*

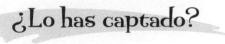

¿Lo has captado?

_____ 1. When Pili says that Pepa has **buen tipo**, she means she has:
   a. good features
   b. a good sense of style
   c. a good figure

_____ 2. Pili thinks Pepa's jacket:
   a. really suits her
   b. is very stylish
   c. is a little tight-fitting

_____ 3. The color of Pepa's jacket is probably:
   a. a little flashy
   b. a little drab
   c. on the pale side

_____ 4. Pepa thinks that Pili's bag is:
   a. really cute
   b. very chic
   c. very exotic

_____ 5. The shop on the calle Fuencarral is probably:
   a. quite expensive
   b. on the trendy side
   c. good for bargains

_____ 6. Pepa and Tom are going to go to:
   a. a Moroccan restaurant
   b. a Moroccan-style nightclub
   c. a Moroccan tea house

_____ 7. When Pili tells Pepa **Te lo vas a pasar bomba**, she means that:
   a. Pepa's going to have a blast
   b. Pepa's going to get very drunk
   c. Pepa's going to flirt with the waiters

Zooming in on appearances and beauty... For better or for worse, appearances are very important in Latin cultures. So we're going to focus here on complimenting others on their looks and possessions, as well as on different terms that denote beauty. Note that there are a few differences between Spain and Latin America, though more often than not the words are universal and it's more a case of common usage and/or local nuances. As a rule, Spanish is harsher and more direct in Spain than in Latin America. *Lindo*, for example, sounds a bit too soft and sweet in Spain, where the spunkier *guapo* is more popular. Meanwhile, *lindo* is very common in Latin America, where people are generally more soft-spoken.

¡Al grano!

Adjectives

bello/a	beautiful (*more common in Latin America*)
bonito/a	nice, beautiful, lovely (*in Spain, used mostly for things*)
chulo/a [col, Spain]	cute, cool, fun (*for things; also common in Mexico, where it means lovely or pretty, and is also used for people*)
divino/a	fabulous, divine
gracioso/a [Spain]	cute, attractive
guapo/a	handsome (*for men*), beautiful (*for women*)
hermoso/a	beautiful (*common in Latin America; in Spain, this often denotes a healthy plumpness, as in babies*)
ideal	beautiful, perfect (*for things*)
lindo/a	nice, beautiful, lovely (*very common in Latin America*)
mono/a [Spain]	cute, pretty
precioso/a	beautiful, gorgeous (*in Spain, used mostly for things*)

Nouns

Note that in English these nouns often translate as adjectives.

una belleza	a knock-out, really beautiful (*used for women*)
una chulada [col, Spain]	really cute, cool (*used for things*)
una hermosura	a knock-out or beauty (*more common in Latin America*)

una monada [Spain]	really cute, adorable (*used mostly for things*)
una preciosidad	really beautiful, gorgeous

More words and expressions

arreglado/a	smart, attractive, well-dressed
horroroso/a	ugly, hideous
llamativo/a	flashy, attention-getting
¿Me ves (tan) horroroso/a (normalmente)? [Spain]	Do I (usually) look (that) awful? (*See "Compliments and Observations" later in this unit.*)
Pareces otro/a	Wow, you look great! (*literally, You look like another person*)
Te favorece	It suits you
tener buen tipo [Spain]	to have a good figure/body
Te queda (muy) bien	It looks (very) good on you (*See "A Catch-All Verb" in Unit 8 for uses of* quedar.)

¡Ojo!

pasarlo bomba [Spain]	to have a great time
Por cierto	By the way
¡Qué envidia!	I'm so jealous! That sounds great!
¿Qué pasa? [col, Spain]	What's up? What's that supposed to mean?
un marroquí/chino/ italiano... [Spain]	a Moroccan/Chinese/Italian restaurant
las rebajas	the sales ([LA] *las liquidaciones* in Argentina and Chile; *las ofertas* in Mexico)
super [col]	very, really

Compliments and Observations

Te veo muy bien

Does this mean *I see you very well?* Well, it can, but it usually means *You're looking really good.* In fact **te veo** + *an adjective*, much like **estás** + *an adjective*, is used often in Spain to compliment someone on his/her appearance.

¡Te veo estupenda! (*or* ¡Estás estupenda!)   You look great!
Te veo muy guapo. (*or* Estás muy guapo.)   You're looking very
                                           handsome.

Te veo radiante.   (*or* Estás radiante.)   You look radiant.

Note, though, that **te veo** + *an adjective* is not just used to comment on someone's physical appearance, but can also convey other impressions you may have of someone at a given moment.

Te veo muy cansada.   You look really tired.
Te veo un poco triste.   You seem a little sad.
Te veo contento.   You look happy.

Also note that in Latin America **te ves** + *an adjective* is more common.

¡Te toca!

To be (**ser**) or *to be* (**estar**)?: that is the question. Which would you use in the following situations? Write a short sentence using an appropriate form of **ser** or **estar**.

1. Compliment a friend on how he/she looks.

    _____

2. Describe a friend or member of your family (either physical traits or personality).

    _____

3. Rave about a city or town you love.

    _____

4. Explain where your favorite restaurant is located.

    _____

5. Compliment a friend on how his/her house (which usually looks as if a bomb had hit it) looks now, after he/she has cleaned and straightened up everything.

    _____

(If you're not sure when to use **ser** or **estar**, reread the dialogue between Pepa and Pili and note how they use them.)

Intercambio

Today Tom has canceled his *intercambio* with Pili to rush off and meet Pepa. They end up taking a walk together through Madrid's Retiro Park. Fill in the blanks as you read their conversation.

Pepa ¡Qué perro más *mono*!

Tom ¡Qué dices! ¡Es un dachshund! No se parece nada a <u>un mono</u>.

Pepa Claro que no. Es que *mono* como adjetivo significa *bonito* o *adorable*...

Tom ¡Ajá! ¿Entonces puedo decir que Marilyn Monroe era

  (1) _____?

Pepa Pues sí, aunque realmente era *más* que mona. Era una

  (2) _____.

Tom Tienes razón. Era una mujer espectacular, explosiva, bellísima...

Pepa Estás un poco obsesionado con Marilyn, ¿no?

Tom Bueno, un poco, pero más contigo. Y <u>hoy eres</u> muy guapa, Pepa.

Pepa Gracias, pero así no se dice. Tendrías que decir (3) _____

  muy guapa hoy o (4) _____ _____ muy guapa.

Tom Ah, ya veo. De todas formas, tú (5) _____ una mujer muy atractiva. En mi opinión aún más atractiva que Marilyn...

Pepa ¡Para ya!, Tom. Estás un poco tremendo hoy.

Tom No, pero es verdad. Y además tienes <u>un cuerpo muy bueno</u>...

Pepa Eso suena fatal, Tom. Se dice más bien que una persona tiene

  (6) _____ _____.

Tom ¡Ajá! Y por cierto, esa camisa (7) _____ _____ muy bien. Estás muy sexy hoy, Pepa.

Pepa Y tú estás un poco pesado...

7

Entra de maravilla

Pepa and Pili savor a little wine

Pili   Oye, Pepa, ya estoy **pedo** y todavía quedan **los crianzas** de Rioja y Ribera del Duero...

Pepa   ¿Pero no oíste al *profe*? *Se trata de* **probar** sólo un poquito y luego **escupirlo**...

Pili   No puedo, Pepa. Lo de **escupir** *me da mucho asco*. Además, está todo tan **rico**...

Pepa   *En todo caso*, el vino **se toma** a **sorbitos**, no a **tragos**. Anda, bébete **un vaso** de agua, que **te entrará muy bien** ahora.

Pili   Lo que **me entró de maravilla** era ese **tinto** chileno. ¡Qué bueno estaba! ¿Te acuerdas del nombre de **la bodega**?

Pepa   No, pero **la cosecha** sí. Era **un reserva** del 95, y sí que estaba buenísimo. Mañana mismo me voy a acercar a **la bodega** a comprar un par de botellas.

Pili   Pues así tendrás algo para **brindar** con Tom. ¿No es su cumpleaños mañana?

Pepa   Es verdad, se me había olvidado. Pues haremos **un brindis** con un vino *como Dios manda*.

Pili   *Di que sí.* Oye Pepa, ¿de verdad no estás un poco **alegre** con todo el vino que **hemos probado**?

Pepa   Pues no. Pero bueno, no he bebido todo lo que me **han echado** en **la copa**, si no estaría **borracha** perdida.

Pili   ¡Qué petarda eres!, Pepa. Una *aguafiestas* total. Venga, pásame esa **jarra** de agua, que me temo que mañana voy a tener **una resaca** brutal.

¿Lo has captado?

_____ 1. Pepa and Pili are:
   a. at a wine bar
   b. in a wine-tasting course
   c. visiting a wine cellar in the Rioja region

_____ 2. At the beginning Pili states that she is:
   a. quite drunk
   b. a little tired
   c. a little confused

_____ 3. The *profe* has told them to:
   a. try a little of each wine, and then spit it out
   b. take a small sip and then swallow the wine
   c. let the wine swill around in their mouths

_____ 4. Pili has been:
   a. spitting the wine out
   b. gulping it down
   c. sipping it

_____ 5. The Chilean wine they tried earlier was:
   a. a dry rosé
   b. a young red
   c. a vintage red

_____ 6. Tomorrow is Tom's birthday and Pepa is going to buy some:
   a. special wine
   b. wine to toast the occasion with
   c. both *a* and *b*

_____ 7. Pili accuses Pepa of being:
   a. a party-pooper
   b. snotty
   c. a teacher's pet

_____ 8. Pili thinks that the next day she will:
   a. get violently sick
   b. have a hangover
   c. take the day off work

Zooming in on wine and drinking . . . We're devoting this unit to wine since, after all, several Spanish-speaking countries (notably Argentina, Chile, and Spain) are major wine producers and wine is closely tied to their culture and customs. In Spain, for example, meals are normally accompanied by wine, and there's a *vino* for every budget and occasion, from a cheap, basic *Valdepeñas* to a choice vintage of *Rioja* or *Ribera del Duero*. Meanwhile, you probably uncork a bottle from time to time too, so all the more reason to look at some common wine-related lingo.

¡Al grano!

alegre	tipsy, merry (*also means cheerful or happy*)
una bodega	a liquor store, a winery, a wine cellar
borracho/a	drunk
brindar	to make a toast
un brindis	a toast
una copa	a glass (*for wine and other alcoholic beverages*)
la cosecha	the vintage or year (*when used in reference to wine*)
un crianza [Spain]	a vintage wine (*a wine that's been aged in oak*)
echar [Spain]	to pour (*for drinks;* [LA] *servir*)
entrar (bien/de maravilla)	to go down (well/great)
escupir	to spit out
una jarra	a pitcher
pedo [col, Spain]	smashed, wasted (*This is also used as a noun. The original meaning of pedo is fart.*)
probar	to try or taste (*for food and drink*)
una resaca	a hangover (*used in many, but not all, Latin American countries*)
un reserva	an old or special vintage (*Note that both crianza and reserva are masculine when used in reference to wine.*)
rico/a	delicious, yummy (*for food and drink*)
un sorbito	a sip (*from sorber, to sip*)
[vino] tinto	red wine
tomar	to have (*for food and drink*)
un trago	a gulp (*tragar = to swallow*)
un vaso	a glass (*for water and nonalcoholic beverages*)

¡Ojo!

un/a aguafiestas	a party-pooper
como Dios manda	the way it's meant to be (*un vino como Dios manda = a real wine*)
Di que sí [col]	Go for it! All right! (*used as an affirmation*)
en todo caso	in any event, anyway
Me da asco	It's disgusting
un/a profe [col, Spain]	teacher (*abbreviated form of profesor/a*)
Se trata de	You're supposed to; It's about . . .

Vintage Expressions

Crianzas y reservas

If you're into wine, you'll probably want to know a few terms that aren't included in the previous lists.

Apart from **vino tinto**, there's also, of course, **vino blanco** and **vino rosado**. Wine is generally **seco** but can also be **dulce** (the latter are usually dessert wines), and in Spain it's said to either **tener crianza** or **no tener crianza**.

If a wine **tiene crianza**, this just means it's been aged in oak, as opposed to **un vino joven** (or **un vino del año**) which hasn't been in an oak barrel and should therefore be drunk within the year. In Spain, a vintage wine (one that's aged in an oak barrel) is either **un crianza** or **un reserva**. **Un crianza** has a life span of five to seven years, while **un reserva** can last up to twenty years (and in some cases longer) and usually gets better with the passage of time. Some wine enthusiasts have **bodegas** in their homes to store **crianzas** and **reservas**.

Meanwhile, wines such as *Rioja* or *Ribera del Duero* have **una denominación de origen**, meaning they're from an officially recognized wine-producing region in Spain. Note here that if you say **La Rioja** you're referring to the region, while **el Rioja** refers to the wine produced in this region. This is because **vino** is masculine and **un Rioja** is basically an abbreviated form of **un vino de La Rioja**. Likewise, **la Reina Sofía** is the current queen of Spain, while **el Reina Sofía** is the museum of modern art in Madrid that's named after her.

Finally, avoid any **vino** in Spain that doesn't have **una denominación de origen**. It'll probably be **peleón** and give you a pretty nasty hangover.

¡Te toca!

Underline the correct word in the sentences below.

1. Este vino **traga** | **entra** | **echa** muy bien.

2. Me gusta más el vino **rojo** | **joven** | **tinto** que el blanco.

3. **Prueba** | **Escupe** | **Trata** este vino. Te va a gustar.

4. Sírveme otra **copa** | **vaso** | **botella** de vino.

5. Vamos a hacer un **sorbito** | **brindis** | **bodega**. ¡Por Juanito!

6. He bebido media botella de vino, y estoy un poco **alegre** | **contento** | **feliz**.

7. ¡Qué rico está este vino! ¿De qué **reserva** | **cosecha** | **crianza** es?

8. Los **crianzas** | **cosechas** | **tintos** tienen más cuerpo que los vinos jóvenes.

Intercambio

It's a balmy summer evening, so Pili and Tom have decided to meet for their *intercambio* today at a *terraza* in the Plaza Santa Ana. Fill in the blanks as you read their dialogue.

Pili   ¿Qué tal, Tom? Te veo muy contento...

Tom   Sí, he encontrado un nuevo trabajo.

Pili   ¡Fantástico! Eso hay que celebrarlo. ¿Tomamos un vinito?

Tom   Sí, un <u>vaso</u> de vino blanco estaría bien.

Pili   Venga, pero se dice una (1) _____ de vino, no *un vaso*.

Tom   ¡Ajá! Pues ¿pedimos un *Rueda*? Me han dicho que es muy bueno y nunca lo he <u>tratado</u>.

Pili   No, Tom, con la comida y bebida se usa el verbo

(2) _____, no *tratar*. ¡Ah!, aquí viene el camarero...

(Cinco minutos más tarde)

Pili   Bueno, Tom, un (3) _____... ¡Por tu nuevo trabajo!

Tom   Mmmm. Este vino está muy rico...

Pili   Tienes razón. (4) _____ muy bien.

Tom   Por cierto, ¿qué tal el curso de vino?

Pili   Bueno, me puse un poco alegre...

Tom   ¡Ah!, entonces fue divertido.

Pili   No exactamente. Es que acabé bastante pedo.

Tom   ¿Pedo? Lo siento, Pili, pero en mi país no hablamos de esas cosas.

Pili   ¡No me has entendido! Es que *alegre* y *pedo* son dos formas de decir

        (5) _____.

Tom   ¡Ajá! Sí, me contó Pepa que bebiste mucho vino <u>rojo</u>...

Pili   Bueno, roja estaba yo, pero el vino era (6) _____.

        Y bueno, al día siguiente tenía una (7) _____ brutal.

8

Una chupa de marca

Pepa and Pili hit the sales

Pili   ¿Qué tal me **quedan** estos **vaqueros**?

Pepa   Un poco **justitos. Una talla** más grande a lo mejor...

Pili   ¡Qué dices! Lo **ceñido** está **de moda**. Mira, **me los quedo,** que están muy **rebajados**.

Pepa   ¡Estás loca! ¡Pero si ya tienes muchísima ropa!

Pili   Oye, Pepa, sólo **voy de compras** en las rebajas, así que *déjame en paz.*

Pepa   Vale, vale, pero venga, no te **pruebes** más cosas.

Pili   Espera, sólo **queda** esta **chupa**. *¡Anda!*, pero si no tiene **etiqueta**...

Pepa   *No pasa nada.* **La dependienta** sabrá qué precio tiene.

Pili   Pues pregúntaselo tú por favor, que *me puso muy mala cara* cuando entré en **el probador**.

Pepa   *No me extraña.* Llevabas diez **prendas** cuando el límite son seis.

Pili   Y ya que vas, pregúntale si **el bolso** que está en **el escaparate** lo tienen en negro.

(Unos minutos más tarde)

Pepa   Cuesta 60 euros tu chaqueta. Un poco **timo**, ¿no te parece?

Pili   Bueno, pero es de **marca**. La relación **calidad-precio** está bien. ¿Y qué te dijo del bolso?

Pepa   Que en negro no **quedan**. Venga, *date prisa*, que van a cerrar la tienda ya.

(Después, en la calle)

Pepa   Escucha, es la última vez que **voy de tiendas** contigo. Y encima está todo cerrado ahora y no puedo **hacer la compra**.

Pili   Tranquila, te invito a comer, ¿vale? Oye, y *¿me echas una mano?* Estas **bolsas** pesan *un huevo*...

¿Lo has captado?

_____ 1. The jeans Pili has tried on are:
   a. a little baqqy
   b. a little tight
   c. just right

_____ 2. Pili decides to get the jeans because:
   a. they're a designer label
   b. they're really marked down
   c. she's going to go on a diet

_____ 3. The jacket Pili wants to try on is missing:
   a. the label
   b. the price tag
   c. a button

_____ 4. Pili tells Pepa that when she went into the changing room, the shop assistant:
   a. gave her a dirty look
   b. went pale
   c. made a nasty comment

_____ 5. This was because Pili:
   a. pushed her by mistake
   b. jumped the line
   c. had too many items of clothing

_____ 6. Pepa thinks the jacket is:
   a. overpriced
   b. a real bargain
   c. too small

_____ 7. Pili thinks the jacket is a good value for the money because:
   a. it has a stain
   b. it's really marked down
   c. it's a designer item

_____ 8. Pepa's pissed off at the end because:
   a. she can't buy groceries
   b. the other clothes stores are closed
   c. she didn't find anything she liked

Zooming in on shopping . . . So you know the basics and how to ask what something costs. But maybe you're not quite sure about the difference between *ir de compras* and *hacer la compra*. And why is a bag sometimes called *un bolso* in Spain and other times *una bolsa*? And what's this *calidad-precio* business? A quality price? And just one more thing: What's *quedar* doing all over the place? Does it have even more meanings? Read on to find the answers as well as more key vocabulary related to rampant consumerism.

¡Al grano!

una bolsa	a large bag (*this includes plastic shopping bags as well as beach bags, travel bags, etc.*)
un bolso [Spain]	a handbag, a purse ([LA] *una cartera; in Mexico,* **una bolsa**)
ceñido/a	close-fitting, clinging
una chupa [col, Spain]	a sports jacket
una marca	a brand (*de marca = a brand name, a designer label*)
de moda	in fashion, "in"
el dependiente/la dependienta	the sales clerk, the shop assistant
un escaparate	a shop window, a window display
la etiqueta	the price tag
hacer la compra	to do the shopping, to buy groceries
ir de compras	to go shopping
ir de tiendas [Spain]	to go shopping
justito/a	tight (*diminutive of justo/a*)
una prenda	an item of clothing
probar	to try on
el probador	the changing room
quedar/quedarse	(*See "A Catch-All Verb" later in this unit.*)
rebajado/a	marked down, on sale
La relación calidad-precio	value for the money (*buena relación calidad-precio = good value, very reasonable*)
una talla	a size
un timo	a rip-off
unos vaqueros [Spain]	jeans ([LA] *jeans*)

¡Ojo!

¡Anda! [Spain]	Hey! Whoa! (*as an exclamation* ***anda*** *expresses surprise—you've just seen, realized, or discovered something*)
¡Date prisa!	Hurry up!
¡Déjame en paz!	Leave me alone! Let me be!
echar una mano	to give a hand, to help out
No me extraña	No wonder; It doesn't surprise me
No pasa nada	No problem; It's no big deal
un huevo [col]	a lot (*vulgar*)
poner mala cara	to pout, grimace, or give a dirty look (*literally, to put on a bad face*)

A Catch-All Verb

Quedar

We looked at *quedar* in Unit 2 and how it's used in Spain to talk about plans. But there's bad news: this verb is used in a lot more ways. In fact, if you looked at the dictionary entry, your eyes might even glaze over. We can't do an exhaustive analysis here, but we will look at four of its most common meanings.

1. to look (*on someone or in a particular place or setting*)

¿Qué tal me *queda* esta chaqueta?	How does this jacket look on me?
Esa mesa va a *quedar* monísima en tu salón.	That table's going to look really cute in your living room.

2. to be (*for "fit" or location*)

Esa camisa te *queda* grande.	That shirt's too big for you.
El aeropuerto *queda* lejos de la ciudad.	The airport's far from the city.

3. to remain or be left

Sólo me *queda* esta chupa.	There's just this jacket left (for me to try on).
Quedan tres días para Navidad.	There are three days (left) to go 'til Christmas.

4. to buy/get or take (*Here you need* **quedarse***, the reflexive form. Note that this is usually used in the present tense and when addressing someone directly.*)

Estos vaqueros *me* **los** *quedo.*	I'm going to get these jeans.
Me quedo **la camisa.**	I'll take the shirt.

¡Te toca!

You're shopping for clothes. Fill in the blanks in this conversation you have with the clerk. (You'll need to use *quedar* three different times here.)

Dependiente   ¿Le puedo ayudar en algo?

Tú   Sí, me podría decir qué (1) _____ tiene esta

camisa. Es que no lleva (2) _____.

Dependiente   Ah sí, me parece que cuesta 15 euros.

Tú   Ajá. ¿Y la tiene en una (3) _____ más grande?

Ésta me (4) _____ un poco pequeña.

Dependiente   Un momento. Ahora lo miro.

(Unos minutos más tarde)

Dependiente   Sí, la tenemos en la L y en la XL. ¿Se quiere

(5) _____ las dos?

Tú   Gracias, no hace falta. Me (6) _____ la L.

Dependiente   Muy bien. Desea algo más?

Tú   Sí. ¿(7) _____ otra chaqueta como la del

(8) _____?

Dependiente   No, lo siento, se han vendido todas.

Tú   Pues nada más. Muchas gracias.

Intercambio

Pili's canceled her *intercambio* with Tom this afternoon so she can hit a few more stores. Meanwhile Pepa meets Tom at his place.

Pepa   ¡Ya está! Es la última vez que voy (1) _____

_____ con Pili.

Tom   ¿Por qué? ¿Qué pasó?

Pepa   Nada, es una pesada. Fíjate, entramos en una tienda a las once de la mañana y no salimos hasta las dos. ¡Tres horas allí dentro!

Tom   ¿Y compró algo?

Pepa   Hombre, se llevó la mitad de la tienda. Tres pares de vaqueros, cinco camisas, dos chaquetas, una chupa...

Tom   ¿Y tú no te compraste nada?

Pepa   No. Me (2) _____ una chaqueta pero no me

(3) _____ bien. Y no me gusta comprar algo sólo porqué

esté (4) _____.

Tom   ¡Ah, es verdad!, son las rebajas ahora. Pues yo necesito un par de camisas...

Pepa   Pues te vas tú solito, guapo.

Tom   Anda, acompáñame, Pepa, que ya sabes que no me gusta nada

(5) _____ _____ compras.

Pepa   Bueno, ya veremos. Por cierto, veo que has hecho

(6) _____ _____.

Tom   Sí, fui al supermercado esta tarde. Y te voy a preparar una cena buenísima...

9

La penúltima...

Pepa and Pili banter at a bar

Pepa   ¡Qué **aceitunas** más buenas!

Pili   Ya te dije que aquí **ponían** unas **tapas** muy ricas. Anda, **prueba** las **patatas bravas** también, que están *que te mueres*.

Pepa   Tienes razón. Y además esta cañita está buenísima.

Pili   Sí, aquí **tiran** la cerveza de miedo.

Pepa   Pues nada, hay que venir más veces a tomar **el aperitivo**.

Pili   Oye, ¿**pedimos** otra cosa para **picar**? ¿**Una ración** de **boquerones en vinagre**, por ejemplo?

Pepa   *Venga...*

Pili   (*Al camarero*) ¡Oiga! **Nos pone** unos boquerones en vinagre **cuando pueda**...

(*Unos minutos después*)

Pepa   Bueno, Pili, ¡vaya **juerga** lo de anoche!

Pili   Sí, estuvo genial. Y ese chico irlandés en el **pub** de Huertas era la monda.

Pepa   ¿El que imitaba a Travolta? Pues **tenía una marcha**... Me agotaba sólo verlo bailar.

Pili   Y a mí... y eso que pensaba que *los guiris* eran *unos muermos* totales.

Pepa   Pues ése desde luego que no. ¿Qué pasa? ¿Te gustó?

Pili   *Un pelín.* En fin, hemos quedado este viernes para **tomar algo por ahí**.

Pepa   ¿Ah sí? Oye, Pili, ¿y tu novio, *qué*?

Pili   ¿Paco? ¡Está todo el rato **de juerga** con sus amigos! ¡*Vete tú a saber*!

Pepa   Pues sí, *se pasa* un poco. En fin, ¿tomamos otra **caña**?

Pili   Vale, **la penúltima**. (*al camarero*) ¡Oiga! Otra **ronda** por favor...

¿Lo has captado?

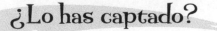

_____ 1. Pepa and Pili are chatting over:
   a. coffee
   b. a drink and snack
   c. dinner

_____ 2. Pili tells Pepa that the *patatas bravas* are:
   a. delicious
   b. overdone
   c. very spicy

_____ 3. The night before Pepa and Pili had gone:
   a. to a party
   b. to a dance contest
   c. out partying on the town

_____ 4. The Irish guy they met at the bar in Huertas was:
   a. a great dancer
   b. really wired
   c. totally drunk

_____ 5. Pili originally thought that foreigners were:
   a. boring
   b. not good dancers
   c. bad at holding their drink

_____ 6. Pili's boyfriend is:
   a. a big party animal
   b. a substance-abuser
   c. a skirt-chaser

_____ 7. At the end, Pepa and Pili agree to have:
   a. another snack
   b. the second-to-last beer
   c. one more beer

Zooming in on bars and nightlife . . . Did you know Spain has more bars per inhabitant than any country in the world? OK, why then do you rarely see any "ugly" drunks? Probably because drinking is usually done socially and in moderation, and is more often than not accompanied by food. Wine, for example, is rarely drunk outside of meals, the *aperitivo* almost always includes a *tapa*, and even hard liquor is often served with nuts or potato chips. As for bars, these break down into two types in Spain: *bares*, which are open all day and also serve coffee, soft drinks, snacks, and meals; and *pubs* (also known as *bares de copas*), which open at night, only serve drinks, and often have a DJ and a dance floor. Below is some vocabulary that will come in handy if you find yourself in any of these establishments.

¡Al grano!

una aceituna	an olive
el aperitivo	an aperitif, a pre-lunch drink and snack (*See "A Spanish Institution" later in this unit.*)
boquerones en vinagre [Spain]	anchovies marinated in vinegar (*common in Spain*)
una caña, cañita [Spain]	a small glass of draft beer (*typical in Madrid*)
Cuando pueda	When you have a moment (*often used when ordering food or drink*)
(estar/ir) de juerga	(to be/to go) out partying and/or clubbing (*See "Out on the Town" later in this unit.*)
una juerga	a blast, a good time, a wild night out on the town
¡Oiga!	Excuse me! (*to get the attention of waiters and bartenders*)
patatas bravas	fried potatoes in a spicy tomato sauce (*typical in Madrid*)
pedir	to order
el/la penúltimo/a	one for the road, the last round (*literally, the second to last*)
picar	to nibble or snack on
poner [Spain]	to serve ([LA] *servir*)
probar	to try or taste
un pub	a music bar that opens at night and serves drinks

una ración [Spain]	a large snack or serving (*una ración de patatas fritas* = *a plate of French fries*)
una ronda	a round (*of drinks*)
una tapa [Spain]	a small snack, usually served before meals
tener marcha [col, Spain]	to be full of energy, into the nightlife or "action" (*See "Out on the Town" later in this unit.*)
tirar	to pull (*in this case, to "pull," or serve, draft beer*)
tomar algo por ahí	to go out for a drink and/or snack

¡Ojo!

un/a guiri [col, Spain]	a foreigner (*generally white and from a non-Latin culture; a little pejorative*)
muermo/a [col, Spain]	boring, someone/something lacking in zest or energy
pasarse	to push it, to go too far
un pelín [col, Spain]	a little
que te mueres [col]	great, fantastic, to "die for"
Venga [col, Spain]	Good idea, OK
¡Vete tú a saber!	Go figure! Your guess is as good as mine . . .
¿Y (tu novio) qué?	What about (your boyfriend)?

A Spanish Institution

El aperitivo

You got it: this is practically an institution in Spain, so it deserves at least a quick mention here. First of all, *el aperitivo* is not just a pre-lunch drink—it almost always involves a snack. Most bars will serve you a free *tapa* or *pincho* (a small morsel or canapé) along with your drink, though *raciones* (which are larger and usually shared among several people) need to be ordered separately. As far as beverages are concerned, the classic choice is a small tumbler of draft beer, known in Madrid as *una caña*, although in Andalusia, *fino* (sherry) is also popular. And be warned: Sunday *aperitivos* have a habit of filling in for lunch and lasting well into the afternoon.

Out on the Town

La juerga y la marcha...

If you're into partying and nightlife, these are two words you'll definitely need in your repertoire. Since neither of them have a real English equivalent, we'll take a closer look at them here.

La juerga. Loosely translated, **una juerga** is a *blast,* a *blowout,* or *a good time.* So *estar de juerga* is to be out partying and having a good time, *ir* or *salir de juerga* is to go out partying or clubbing, and *un/a juerguista* is a party animal or someone that likes being out and about socializing and partying.

La marcha [col, Spain]. This conveys the idea of liveliness and energy, usually in reference to nightlife and partying. So if a neighborhood *tiene marcha*, this means it's lively at night, and *una persona marchosa* (or *una persona que tiene marcha*) is someone who's full of energy and into the nightlife or "action."

¡Te toca!

Fill in the blanks using the words below.

tomar	picar	aperitivo	ración
tapa	ronda	juerga	marcha

1. No tengo mucha _____ hoy. Me voy a quedar en casa.

2. ¿Pido otra _____ de cervezas?

3. En muchos bares te ponen una _____ cuando pides una bebida.

4. Me encanta tomar el _____ los domingos.

5. ¿Quedamos el viernes para _____ algo por ahí?

6. Salí de _____ anoche, y hoy estoy muy cansado.

7. ¿Tomamos una _____ de queso manchego?

8. ¿Pedimos unas aceitunas para _____?

Intercambio

Pili's canceled her *intercambio* with Tom again, since she was out the night before and is not feeling in top form. Meanwhile, Tom and Pepa decide to go out for an *aperitivo*. Fill in the blanks as you read their dialogue.

Tom   ¡Qué sed tengo!

Pepa   Yo también. Una cañita va a entrar muy bien ahora.

Tom   ¿Pedimos algo para (1) _____ también?

Pepa   Por supuesto. Además tienen unos pinchos muy ricos aquí.

Tom   A ver, ¿qué recomiendas?

Pepa   Pues mira, los canapés de salmón están que (2) _____ _____.

Tom   ¡Ah!, pues me gusta mucho el salmón...

Pepa   ¡Ah!, mira, allí está el camarero. ¿Por qué no (3) _____ tú?

Tom   Vale. *(al camarero)* ¡(4) _____! ¿Nos (5) _____ dos cañas y dos canapés de salmón, por favor?

(Diez minutos más tarde)

Pepa   Por cierto, Tom, ¿qué te ha dicho Pili? ¿Por qué ha cancelado el intercambio hoy?

Tom   Estaba muy cansada. Creo que salió de (6) _____ anoche.

Pepa   Es verdad, quedó ayer con el irlandés para (7) _____ algo por ahí.

Tom   ¿Qué irlandés?

Pepa   Pues uno que le gusta un poco. Oye, ¿tomamos otra caña?

Tom   Vale, una por el camino...

Pepa   ¡Por el camino! Pero ¿no prefieres tomarla aquí?

Tom   Claro. Quiero decir la última...

Pepa   ¡Ah! ¡La (8) _____! Pues venga...

¡Nos vamos a forrar!

Pili's strapped for cash

Pili   Pepa, ¿me puedes **prestar** 50 euros? **Estoy sin un duro.**

Pepa   Pero ¿no acabas de **cobrar** hace unos días?

Pili   Sí, pero me he gastado **una pasta** en las rebajas. Bueno, y *ni te cuento lo de* mi **factura** de teléfono. Casi me da un ataque.

Pepa   Claro... ¡*A quién se le ocurre* tener un novio en Irlanda!

Pili   *Eso es asunto mío*, guapa. Anda, te los **devolveré** la semana que viene.

Pepa   Toma, 50 euros... Aunque eres *boba*, tenías que haberte quedado con el otro, que estaba **forrado.**

Pili   Bueno, *iba de* rico pero **nunca llevaba nada encima.** De hecho, *íbamos a medias* casi siempre.

Pepa   Vaya, **un tacaño**, ¡lo peor! Aunque eso de **pagar cada uno lo suyo** es bastante normal hoy en día.

Pili   *Ya*, pero los tíos **ganan** más y encima no tienen **gastos.** Como viven todos en casa de sus padres...

Pepa   Tienes razón. Son *unos sinvergüenzas.*

Pili   Oye, Pepa, ¿y cómo es que tú nunca **estás mal de dinero**?

Pepa   Porque **ingreso** una parte de mi **sueldo** en **una cuenta de ahorros** que sólo toco en momentos de **apuro.**

Pili   ¡Qué **previsora**! En fin, Pepa, estoy harta de **estar** siempre **en la miseria.**

Pepa   Pues **apriétate el cinturón** y **ahorra** un poco, chica.

Pili   No puedo. Tengo una idea mejor. Vamos a jugar a la lotería...

Pepa   ¡No seas tonta! Eso es **tirar el dinero.**

Pili   Oye, nunca se sabe... Venga, Pepa, ¡**nos vamos a forrar**!

¿Lo has captado?

———— 1. Pili asks Pepa to lend her 50 euros although she:
  - a. has some savings
  - b. just got paid
  - c. just took out a personal loan

———— 2. Pili is broke because she:
  - a. made a lot of long distance calls
  - b. splurged on the sales
  - c. both *a* and *b*

———— 3. Pepa tells Pili she's an idiot to have:
  - a. run up her phone bill
  - b. gone to Ireland
  - c. left her previous boyfriend

———— 4. Pili's ex-boyfriend was:
  - a. a leech
  - b. a cheapskate
  - c. a big spender

———— 5. Pepa thinks that:
  - a. going Dutch is pretty common now
  - b. Pili's paying for her past mistakes
  - c. the man should always treat

———— 6. Pepa is always solvent because she:
  - a. isn't an impulse buyer
  - b. has an emergency fund
  - c. is very frugal

———— 7. Pepa's advice to Pili is to:
  - a. buy fewer clothes
  - b. stop playing the lottery
  - c. put some money aside

Zooming in on money . . . Euros are in, pesetas are history, and no doubt this will get reflected in the language down the line. Perhaps *estoy sin un duro* will become *estoy sin un euro*, but it just doesn't roll off the tongue as well, and for now the expression is showing no signs of dying out. Currency matters aside, the core words and expressions you'll need to talk about money are not going to change.

¡Al grano!

ahorrar	to save
apretarse el cinturón	to tighten one's belt, to economize
apuro	financial need, hardship (*en momentos de apuro* = *when I'm hard up*)
cobrar	to get paid
una cuenta de ahorros	a savings account
devolver	to pay back
estar mal de dinero	to be hard up, to have money problems (*See "Pleading Poverty" later in this unit.*)
estar en la miseria [Spain]	to be broke (*See "Pleading Poverty" later in this unit.*)
estar sin un duro [col, Spain]	to be broke (*See "Pleading Poverty" later in this unit.*)
una factura	a bill, an invoice
forrado/a [col]	loaded, rolling in it, very rich (*only used in some Latin American countries*)
forrarse [Spain]	to get rich
ganar	to earn or win
gastos	expenses (*from gastar, to spend*)
ingresar [Spain]	to deposit (into an account) ([LA] *depositar*)
ir a medias [Spain]	to go fifty-fifty, to go Dutch
no llevar nada encima	not to have any money on you
pagar cada uno lo suyo	to pay one's share
pasta [col, Spain]	money (*una pasta* = *a fortune, a lot of money*; [LA] *plata*)
prestar	to lend
previsor/a	prudent, sensible
un sueldo	a salary
(un/a) tacaño/a	(*n*) cheapskate, miser; (*adj*) stingy, tight-fisted
tirar el dinero	to throw money out the window

¡Ojo!

¿A quién se le ocurre...?	Who'd ever think of . . . ?
bobo/a	silly, stupid
Eso es asunto mío	That's my business
ir de (rico)	to act like one's (rich)
un/a sinvergüenza	a shameless person; someone with "nerve"
Ya [Spain]	Yes, I know
Y ni te cuento lo de...	And I'm not even going to go into . . .

Pleading Poverty

Estoy sin un duro

What if, against all our predictions, **estar sin un duro** becomes obsolete down the line? No problem. You still have all these expressions to fall back on when you're strapped for cash.

Estoy en la miseria [Spain]
Estoy en la quiebra
Estoy en la ruina *or* **estoy arruinado/a**
Estoy mal/fatal de dinero
Estoy sin blanca [col, Spain]
Estoy sin pasta [col, Spain]
Estoy sin un pavo [col, Spain]
Estoy sin plata [LA]

¡Te toca!

Replace the words in italics with a word or expression from the list below.

sin un duro	está forrada	una pasta	apretarme el cinturón
ir a medias	pasta	he cobrado	se forró

1. Me costó *una fortuna*. _____

2. La reina de Inglaterra *es muy rica*. _____

3. ¿Me puedes prestar algo? Estoy *fatal de dinero*. _____

4. No me invites. Vamos a *pagar cada uno lo suyo*. _____

5. Mucha gente *se hizo rica* en los años noventa. _____

6. Si tuviese un poco de *dinero*, me compraría un DVD.

   _____

7. Este mes voy a *gastar menos* y ahorrar un poco.

   _____

8. No *me han pagado* todavía. _____

Intercambio

Pepa and Pili didn't win the lottery, and Pepa's loan isn't enough to get Pili through the month. So Pili's broke again by the time she meets up with Tom for their *intercambio*. Fill in the blanks as you read their dialogue.

Tom   Hola, Pili. ¿Qué tal?

Pili   Pues mira, fatal. (1) _____ en la miseria.

Tom   ¿Estás triste? ¿Qué ocurre?

Pili   ¡Que estoy sin un duro, Tom! ¿No lo entiendes?

Tom   ¿Sin un duro? ¿Qué quiere decir eso?

Pili   Es una expresión. Es que este mes he tenido muchos

      (2) _____ y estoy muy mal (3) _____ _____.

Tom   ¡Ah! Ya entiendo. Oye, si quieres te puedo (4) _____ algo.

Pili   ¿No te importa? Te lo (5) _____ el mes que viene.

Tom   No te preocupes. ¿Te doy 100 euros? ¿Está bien?

Pili   Gracias, Tom. Eres un cielo.

Tom   De nada. Oye, y hoy no <u>vamos al holandés</u>, ¿vale?

Pili   ¿Al holandés? ¿Y a qué holandés íbamos a ir?

Tom   No, quería decir que hoy tú no pagas nada.

Pili   ¡Ah! ¡Que no vamos a (6) _____!

Tom   Exacto. Invito yo. Además soy rico. <u>Estuve pagado</u> ayer.

Pili   Quieres decir que (7) _____ ayer...

Tom   Ajá. Además me han subido el (8) _____ este mes...

Pili   ¿Ah sí? ¡Qué bien! Entonces, ¡estás forrado!

11

Estoy a tope

Pili's snowed under at work

Pili   *No puedo más*, Pepa. Necesito **unas vacaciones**.

Pepa   Y yo... Esto de **currar** tanto no es sano.

Pili   *¡Ni que lo digas!* Llevo *una racha* que **no paro**. Hoy he pasado toda la mañana *pegada al* **ordenador** sin descansar.

Pepa   ¿Y tus **compañeros de trabajo**? ¿También están **agobiados**?

Pili   *¡Qué va!* Yo **estoy a tope** y ellos están allí charlando. **No dan ni golpe.**

Pepa   Vaya... ¿Y qué tal la nueva chica que acabáis de **contratar**?

Pili   ¿Ésa? ¡Es **una enchufada**! La **han cogido** porque su padre es amigo del presidente. Y se pasa el día **haciendo la pelota** al **jefe**. Es para vomitar, tía...

Pepa   Desde luego...

Pili   En fin, *estoy hasta el gorro* del **trabajo**. Y no aguanto más a mi **jefe**.

Pepa   ¿Qué dices? Siempre te has llevado bien con Arturo...

Pili   Sí, pero desde que le han **ascendido** y es **un pez gordo** en **la empresa**, se ha puesto insoportable.

Pepa   Vaya...

Pili   *Total*, chica, estoy super **quemada**. A ver si consigo que me **despidan**.

Pepa   Y si te **echan**, ¿qué harías? ¿Vivirías del **paro**?

Pili   Pues claro, mientras que **me organizo**. Y luego a lo mejor me **monto un negocio**. Algo **rentable**, claro.

Pepa   ¡Estás loca! ¿Y cómo lo harías? No tienes **capital**...

Pili   Eso *es lo de menos*... Ya verás, Pepa, ¡voy a **triunfar**!

¿Lo has captado?

_____ 1. Today Pili spent the entire morning:
   a. filing
   b. on the computer
   c. making phone calls

_____ 2. When Pili says that her coworkers **no dan ni golpe**, this means they:
   a. gossip a lot
   b. don't meet deadlines
   c. sit around doing nothing

_____ 3. Pili complains that she is:
   a. underemployed
   b. snowed under with work
   c. under pressure from her boss

_____ 4. The new employee in Pili's office was hired because of:
   a. her looks
   b. her people skills
   c. a contact high up in the company

_____ 5. Pili got along well with her boss until he:
   a. got a promotion
   b. became a workaholic
   c. started acting strange

_____ 6. Pili wants to:
   a. get a raise
   b. get laid off
   c. take a vacation

_____ 7. At the end, Pili announces that she's going to:
   a. go into real estate
   b. set up her own business
   c. rent office space

Zooming in on work... Let's be honest: the Spanish have tradi-
tionally seen work as a private little corner of their lives that's best
not dwelled on. This is probably related to the fact that what you do
is less important than who you are (your personality) in most Latin
cultures. Also, a little advice: don't come straight out and ask what
someone does for a living when you've just met them. It's considered
gauche and invasive. Still, to get into the general spirit of things,
you'll need some vocabulary to complain that you're overworked,
fed up with your boss or coworkers, and deserve a promotion and/or
vacation.

¡Al grano!

agobiado/a	overwhelmed, overloaded (*very common in Spain*)
ascender	to promote, to give a promotion
coger [Spain]	to hire (*Note that coger, which usually means "to get," is very common in Spain, but completely taboo in Latin America.*)
un/a compañero/a de trabajo	a coworker, a workmate
contratar	to hire
currar [col, Spain]	to work (*el curro = work*)
despedir	to lay off or dismiss
echar	to lay off or fire
una empresa	a company
un/a enchufado/a [col, Spain]	a person who was hired because of a contact
estar hasta el gorro [Spain]	to have had it; to be fed up (*literally, to be up to one's cap; see "Letting off Steam" later in this unit*)
estar a tope [col, Spain]	to be very busy
hacer la pelota [Spain]	to brownnose or try to ingratiate oneself
el jefe/la jefa	the boss
montar un negocio [Spain]	to set up a business ([syn] *poner un negocio*)
no dar ni golpe	to do nothing; to be idle
no parar	to be very busy (*literally, to not stop*)
un ordenador [Spain]	a computer ([LA] *una computadora or un computador*)
organizarse	to get one's act together
el paro [Spain]	unemployment (*vivir del paro = to live off unemployment*)

pegado/a (al ordenador, a la tele...)	glued (to the computer, the TV . . .)
un pez gordo	a big shot, a VIP (*literally, a fat fish*)
quemado/a [col, Spain]	burned out
rentable	profitable
triunfar	to "make it," to be very successful
unas vacaciones	a vacation

¡Ojo!

Es lo de menos	That's the least of it; That doesn't matter
¡Ni que lo digas! [Spain]	You said it; I'll second that
No puedo más	I've had it
¡Qué va!	Ha! On the contrary!
una racha	a period, spell, stretch of time ([Spain] *Llevo una racha que no paro* = *I've been really busy lately*)
Total	Anyway; To sum things up

Letting off Steam

¡Estoy hasta el gorro!

You've had it with your boss, your coworkers, your job . . . or anyone or anything for that matter. Here are some more expressions you can use when you've been pushed to your limits and just can't take it anymore.

¡Estoy hasta los cojones!	*Vulgar; since the reference is to male genitals, this is mostly used by men*
¡Estoy hasta la coronilla!	*Literally, I'm up to the crown of my head*
¡Estoy hasta el moño! [Spain]	*Since the reference is to a hair bun, this is mostly used by women*
¡Estoy hasta las narices! [Spain]	*Literally, I'm up to my noses*

¡Te toca!

What would you say in the following situations? Match each item with a statement or comment from the list below.

_____ 1. You just got a promotion.

_____ 2. Your boss is number two in the company.

_____ 3. You're working round the clock.

_____ 4. Your coworkers are lazy bums.

_____ 5. The new guy is the boss' nephew.

_____ 6. A coworker just got laid off.

_____ 7. You've had it with your job.

_____ 8. Your little niece is really smart and motivated.

_____ 9. You're going to set up your own business.

_____ 10. A coworker is complimenting the boss.

a. **No dan ni golpe.**

b. **Lo han echado.**

c. **Va a triunfar.**

d. **Es un enchufado.**

e. **Le está haciendo la pelota.**

f. **Voy a montar un negocio.**

g. **Estoy a tope.**

h. **Es un pez gordo.**

i. **Estoy hasta el gorro.**

j. **Me han ascendido.**

Intercambio

Several days later, Tom and Pili meet up for their *intercambio*. Fill in the blanks as you read their dialogue.

Pili Bueno, Tom, cuéntame un poco de tu nuevo trabajo...

Tom ¡Ah!, todo bien. Me gusta la empresa y me llevo bien con mi

(1) _____.

Pili ¡Qué bien!

Tom Sí, y el mes que viene creo que me van

a (2) _____ .

Pili No me extraña. Eres muy trabajador y sabes hacer la pelota muy bien.

Tom   Bueno, mi empresa fabrica pelotas, pero yo trabajo en relaciones públicas.

Pili   Ya lo sé, Tom, no me refería a eso. *Hacer la pelota* es querer caer bien a los que están por encima de ti. Tu jefe, por ejemplo, u los

(3) _____ ____ _____ de la empresa.

Tom   ¡Ajá! Pues es importante tener buenas relaciones con tu jefe si quieres avanzar.

Pili   Desde luego. Y seguro que tienes un buen futuro allí. ¿No me dijiste que tu empresa se estaba forrando con esas pelotas?

Tom   Si, se venden muy bien. Es un negocio muy (4) _____.
Y ahora mismo tengo mucho trabajo. La verdad es que no

(5) _____.

Pili   Mejor, así no te aburres.

Tom   No, pero es demasiado. Creo que voy a (6) _____ una persona para ayudarme.

Pili   Pero, ¿no tienes ya a alguien?

Tom   Sí, pero no da ni (7) _____. Lo van a (8) _____, creo.

Pili   Vaya. Por cierto, ¿no tienes vacaciones dentro de poco?

Tom   Sí, en noviembre. Y ¿sabes qué? Pepa y yo nos vamos al Yucatán...

12

¡Qué chollo!

Pepa and Pili haggle at the Rastro

Pepa	Cuidado con tu bolso, que hay dos **chorizos** detrás.
Pili	¿Ah sí? Pues ya me han robado una vez en **el Rastro**, y si lo intentan otra vez, *se van a enterar*.
Pepa	Estamos *a salvo*. *Se han pirado*.
Pili	Oye, Pepa, ¡qué mesa más chula! ¿La ves?
Pepa	Sí, es bonita. Anda, pregunta cuánto **piden por** ella.
Pili	Venga, **ahora vuelvo**.

(Dos minutos después)

Pili	150 euros. Carísima, ¿no?
Pepa	**Un robo**, tía. Venga, ofrécele la mitad y a ver lo que te dice.
Pili	¡Que no!, Pepa. Yo *no valgo para* el **regateo**.
Pepa	Pues, déjalo entonces. ¿*Nos damos una vuelta* y vemos más **puestos**?
Pili	¡Espera! ¿Crees que de verdad **me bajaría el precio**?
Pepa	*Por intentarlo no pierdes nada*.
Pili	Bueno, pero acompáñame y me ayudas a **discutir el precio**, ¿vale?

(Se acercan al vendedor)

Pepa	Escuche, si **nos la da por** 75 euros, **nos la llevamos**.
Vendedor	Le cuento, señorita, esta mesa es **antigua**. Era de mis **bisabuelos**.
Pepa	*¡Anda ya!* **No me engañe**, que es de pino y no tiene más de diez años.
Vendedor	Mire, **se la dejo** a su amiga **en un precio especial**. Deme 100 euros y **estamos en paz**.
Pepa	Que no. 80 euros, **última oferta**. Vámonos, Pili, que veo más mesas por allí...
Vendedor	*Está bien*, *está bien*, deme 85...

(Unos minutos después)

Pili	Bueno, **tirada**, tía. ¡Qué chollo!
Pepa	Sí, ha sido **una ganga** al final. Y esta mesita va a *quedar* monísima en tu salón.

¿Lo has captado?

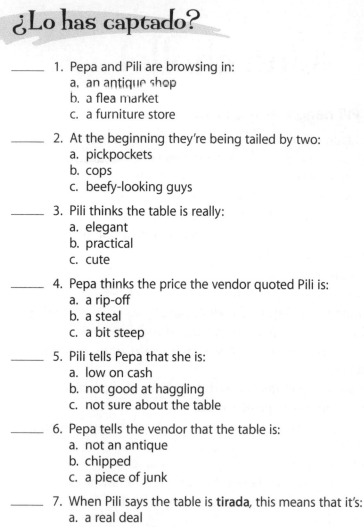

_____ 1. Pepa and Pili are browsing in:
  a. an antique shop
  b. a flea market
  c. a furniture store

_____ 2. At the beginning they're being tailed by two:
  a. pickpockets
  b. cops
  c. beefy-looking guys

_____ 3. Pili thinks the table is really:
  a. elegant
  b. practical
  c. cute

_____ 4. Pepa thinks the price the vendor quoted Pili is:
  a. a rip-off
  b. a steal
  c. a bit steep

_____ 5. Pili tells Pepa that she is:
  a. low on cash
  b. not good at haggling
  c. not sure about the table

_____ 6. Pepa tells the vendor that the table is:
  a. not an antique
  b. chipped
  c. a piece of junk

_____ 7. When Pili says the table is **tirada**, this means that it's:
  a. a real deal
  b. good value for the money
  c. a vintage piece

Zooming in on bargaining . . . We dealt with shopping earlier. But what if an item you want has a crack, tear, or some other flaw? Or you like bargain-hunting in outdoor flea markets? Or you're in Guatemala or Mexico (or any place with a thriving arts and crafts tradition) and you're trying to get a vendor to come down a little? Or you're negotiating the price of your future house, car, or a vase that's caught your eye in an antique store? Here's some vocabulary that will come in handy when the situation calls for a little haggling.

¡Al grano!

Ahora vuelvo	I'll be right back
antiguo/a	antique, old (*versus* **viejo/a,** *which often has negative connotations*)
bajar el precio	to bring down the price (**subir el precio** = *to hike up the price*)
un chollo [col, Spain]	a great deal
un chorizo [col, Spain]	a small-time crook, a pickpocket
dar por *or* dejar en	to sell for (**Se lo doy por 10 euros** *or* **Se la dejo en 10 euros** = *I'll give it to you for 10 euros*)
discutir el precio	to haggle, to argue over the price
engañar (a alguien)	to deceive or trick (someone)
Estamos en paz	We're quits; We're even
una ganga	a bargain
llevarse (algo)	to take (something) (**Me la llevo** = *I'll take it*)
pedir (por algo)	to ask (for something)
un precio especial	a special price, a good deal
un puesto	a stall
el Rastro	the outdoor flea market in Madrid
regatear	to bargain, to haggle
el regateo	bargaining, haggling
un robo [col]	a rip-off; too expensive (*from* **robar,** *to rob or to steal*)
tirado/a [col, Spain]	a steal ([syn] **regalado/a**)
última oferta	last offer
un/a vendedor/a	a vendor

¡Ojo!

¡Anda ya! [Spain]	Come on! Don't give me that!
a salvo	safe
los bisabuelos	great-grandparents
dar una vuelta	to take a stroll, to go for a walk
Está bien	All right, OK
pirarse [col, Spain]	to beat it, to split, to leave quickly
Por intentarlo no pierdes nada	You've got nothing to lose by trying
Queda (bien, mono, ideal...)	It looks (good, cute, great . . .)
	(*See "A Catch-All Verb" in Unit 8.*)
Se van a enterar... [col, Spain]	They're gonna get it; They've got it coming . . .
valer para (algo)	to be good at (something)

¡Te toca!

A. You're browsing in a thrift shop and a ceramic plate catches your eye. Fill in the blanks in the conversation you have with the store owner.

Tú   Perdón. ¿Cuánto (1) _____ este plato?

Vendedor   50 euros. Es una pieza antigua de Talavera.

Tú   Sí, es bonito, pero me parece muy (2) _____.

            ¿No me podría (3) _____ el precio un poco?

Vendedor   Bueno, se lo podría (4) _____ en 45 euros.

Tú   Si me lo (5) _____ por 40, me lo (6) _____.

Vendedor   Deme 42 euros, y estamos en (7) _____.

B. Replace the words in italics with a synonym from below.

regatear	cuesta	una ganga	un precio especial
un robo	tirada	doy por	llevo

1. Me parece *carísimo*. _____

2. No quiero *discutir el precio*. _____

3. Es *un chollo*. _____

4. Voy a preguntar cuánto *piden por* esa jarra. _____

5. Es un poco caro, pero me lo *quedo*. _____

6. En las rebajas puedes encontrar ropa *muy barata*. _____

7. Se lo *dejo en* 20 euros. _____

8. Al final me hizo *un descuento*. _____

Intercambio

Today Pili and Tom have met for their *intercambio* in the Rastro, Madrid's outdoor flea market. Fill in the blanks as you read their dialogue.

Tom ¿Venden lámparas (1) _____ aquí?

Pili ¿Qué tipo de lámpara buscas?

Tom Una lámpara "art deco." Me gustan mucho.

Pili Pues igual tienen alguna en una de las tiendas de antigüedades ahí abajo.

Tom ¿Estará más barata allí que en otras tiendas?

Pili Lo dudo. En fin, antes encontrabas cosas tiradas en el Rastro, pero hoy en día no hay tantas

(2) _____.

Tom Pero me contó Pepa lo de tu mesa. Era un robo, ¿no?

Pili Todo lo contrario. Era un (3) _____.

Tom Sí, eso es lo que quería decir. Era muy barata.

Pili Pues sí, gracias a Pepa. Me ayudó a (4) _____ el precio.

Tom ¡Ajá! Pues me ayudas tú ahora, ¿vale? ¿Sabes (5) _____?

Pili No, lo hago fatal, Tom. Además cuando vean que eres americano, nos van a intentar (6) _____.

Tom Entonces, ¿qué hacemos?

Pili Pues nada, nos damos una (7) _____ por el Rastro, y vuelves otro día con Pepa. Es la reina del regateo...

13

Unas vacaciones de cine

Pepa tells Pili about her Yucatan odyssey

Pili   ¿Así que viste muchas ruinas mayas?

Pepa   Claro, nos **recorrimos** todo el Yucatán.

Pili   ¿Y este edificio? ¡Qué bonito!

Pepa   Ah sí, eso es Mérida. Fuimos primero allí para **visitar la ciudad** y **ver los monumentos**. Y desde allí **hicimos** toda **la ruta maya**.

Pili   ¡Qué envidia! ¿Y cómo **os desplazasteis** de un sitio a otro?

Pepa   Pues era **complicado**. Como no fuimos en **un viaje organizado**, **nos movíamos** al principio en los autobuses locales. Pero era *un rollo*, y entonces **alquilamos** un coche.

Pili   ¿Ah sí? Pero bueno, no **condujo** Tom, espero...

Pepa   Un poco al principio y casi nos mata. El resto del viaje estuvo de **copiloto**.

Pili   Menos mal. Porque si encima *le dabais al* tequila...

Pepa   *¡Qué va!* No bebíamos casi nada. Y nos acostábamos pronto todos los días para **aprovechar las horas de luz** y hacer **excursiones**.

Pili   Oye, ¿y esta playa?, Pepa. *¡Qué pasada!*

Pepa   Ah sí, está en Tulum.

Pili   ¿Y los turistas? Parece que *no hay ni un alma*.

Pepa   Es que es una **zona** muy **virgen** y la costa no está nada **explotada**. Aparte de que era **temporada baja**. Por eso también **el vuelo** nos salió tan barato.

Pili   Pues habréis tenido unas vacaciones *de cine*. ¡Pero bueno!, Pepa... ¿Cuántos **carretes** usaste?

Pepa   Creo que cinco. *Quedan por* revelar otros tres.

Pili   ¡Qué tremenda eres!, *hija*. ¡Ay!, y qué graciosa esta foto de Tom comiendo guacamole. Parece un *gringo* total...

¿Lo has captado?

_____ 1. Pepa and Pili are looking at:
  a. photos
  b. slides
  c. a home video

_____ 2. At first Pepa and Tom were in Mérida:
  a. visiting a friend
  b. sightseeing
  c. both *a* and *b*

_____ 3. Pepa tells Pili that she and Tom:
  a. weren't very organized
  b. had a very complicated itinerary
  c. didn't go on a package tour

_____ 4. During the trip Tom:
  a. drove a lot
  b. didn't drive at all
  c. drove a little

_____ 5. During the trip Pepa and Tom probably:
  a. slept a lot
  b. had jet lag
  c. got up very early

_____ 6. From Pepa's comments, we know that the beach near Tulum
  was:
  a. totally unspoiled
  b. empty
  c. both *a* and *b*

_____ 7. Pepa and Tom went to the Yucatan in:
  a. low season
  b. high season
  c. the hurricane season

_____ 8. Pili thinks the snapshot of Tom is:
  a. not very flattering
  b. hilarious
  c. terrible

Zooming in on travel . . . Chances are if you got this book you're beyond basic survival Spanish, don't have problems dealing with travel agents and hotel staff, and are more interested in really communicating with people. So whether you're planning a trip for the near future or are already roaming or even residing in a Spanish-speaking country, here's some travel-related vocabulary you can use to tell your *amigos* all about your trips, excursions, and weekend escapades.

¡Al grano!

alquilar (un coche, etc.)	to rent or hire (a car, *etc.*) ([LA] *rentar* is used in many Latin American countries)
aprovechar	to take advantage of
un carrete [Spain]	a roll of film ([LA] *un rollo*)
conducir [Spain]	to drive ([LA] *manejar*)
el copiloto	the person in the passenger seat, the navigator
desplazarse	to get from one place to another
una excursión	a day trip, an excursion
explotado/a	developed
hacer la ruta (maya/románica/ del vino...)	to do the (Mayan, Romanesque, wine . . .) route
las horas de luz	daylight hours
moverse	to get around
recorrer	to tour, travel around
revelar	to develop (photographs, film)
temporada baja/alta	low/high season
ver los monumentos	to see the sights
un viaje organizado	a package tour (*generally including accommodations, local travel arrangements, and sightseeing tours*)
virgen	unspoiled, natural, wild (*una playa virgen* = *an unspoiled beach*)
visitar la ciudad	to visit a city, to go sightseeing
un vuelo	a flight
una zona	an area

¡Ojo!

darle (a algo)	to consume repeatedly (*darle al tequila* = *to knock back tequilas*)
de cine [col, Spain]	fantastic ([syn] *de película*)
un/a gringo/a [LA]	an American or foreigner of Anglo-Saxon descent
hijo/a [Spain]	kiddo
No hay ni un alma	There isn't a soul; It's totally deserted
¡Qué pasada! [col, Spain]	Wow! That's amazing!
un rollo [col, Spain]	a drag, a pain in the neck
Quedan (tres) por (revelar)	There are (three) left (to develop) (*See "A Catch-All Verb" in Unit 8.*)

¡Te toca!

Underline the word that best completes the sentence.

1. Es una zona muy **virgen** | **turística** | **explotada**. Casi no hay gente.

2. Siempre viajo en **ruta** | **estación** | **temporada** baja porque es más barato y hay menos gente.

3. Estuvimos en la costa pero hicimos muchas **visitas** | **excursiones** | **recorridos** al interior.

4. Si quieres ir a la China, te recomiendo que vayas en un viaje **aprovechado** | **organizado** | **recorrido**.

5. Como no conduzco, siempre estoy de **carrete** | **copiloto** | **turista**.

6. Con un día en Segovia tienes tiempo suficiente para ver los **monumentos** | **vistas** | **lugares**.

7. El año que viene voy a hacer la **excursión** | **ruta** | **ruina** románica por Palencia.

Intercambio

Tom and Pili meet a few days later for their *intercambio*. Fill in the blanks as you read their dialogue.

Pili   ¿Te gustó México?

Tom   Sí, fue genial. ¿Has visto las fotos?

Pili   Sí, aunque quedaba algún carrete

por (1) _____. En fin, ¡qué envidia! Hicisteis toda la

(2) _____ maya, ¿no?

Tom   Casi toda. Pero creo que la próxima vez

iremos en un viaje (3) _____.

Pili   Ah sí, me dijo Pepa que tuvisteis problemas con el transporte local.

Pero luego (4) _____ un coche, ¿no?

Tom   No me lo recuerdes por favor. Casi nos mata un loco en la carretera.

Pili   ¿Ah sí? ¿Qué pasó?

Tom   Nada, los mejicanos (5) _____ como kamikazes. Peor aún que los españoles.

Pili   ¡Anda ya! Es que en los Estados Unidos sois un rollo. Vais muy lento.

Tom   Eso dice Pepa también. Total, estuve el resto del viaje de

(6) _____.

Pili   Mejor, así se disfruta más del paisaje.

Tom   Es verdad.

Pili   Bueno, y esa playa donde fuisteis... ¡qué pasada! Y encima estabais allí solos...

Tom   Es que esa zona no está nada (7) _____. Y claro,

también era (8) _____ baja.

Pili   ¡Qué envidia! Bueno, y la comida mejicana, ¿qué tal?

Tom   Que te mueres...

14

¡Estás como una foca!

Pili needs to lose a pound or two

Pepa   Oye, esa **tripita** no la tenías antes, Pili.

Pili   Ni estos **michelines**... Bueno, y lo peor es que ya **no entro en** la ropa.

Pepa   Pues sí, ¡**estás como una foca**!, chica.

Pili   ¡Por favor!, Pepa. *Como mucho*, **he engordado** cinco kilos.

Pepa   Ya, pero como **eres de constitución** delgada, *se te nota* más. Mira, no pasa nada. **Te pones a régimen** y en un mes **bajas de peso**.

Pili   Pues mañana mismo voy a empezar una dieta macrobiótica.

Pepa   ¡No seas tan radical! *Basta con* **quitarte** la cerveza y el pan y **hacer** un poco de **vida sana**. Ya sabes, mucha **verdurita** y pescado y poca **grasa**.

Pili   Bueno, ya veremos. ¡Ah!, por cierto, **me he apuntado a** un gimnasio.

Pepa   ¿Ah sí? Pues ya verás, no hay nada como hacer ejercicio para sentirte bien y ponerte **en forma**.

Pili   Tienes toda la razón. Hoy fui a la clase de aeróbic y estuve una hora **pegando saltos** y **sudando** *como una bestia*. Y luego *me metí en* el **baño turco**. Es *una gozada*, tía. **Sales como nueva**.

Pepa   Claro, es que así eliminas *un montón* de toxinas.

Pili   Bueno, y después está el gimnasio lleno de tíos **cachas**. Todos allí andando en **la cinta** y **haciendo pesas**.

Pepa   Pensé que no te gustaban los tíos muy musculosos.

Pili   Pues *tipo* Schwarzenegger no, pero así un poco **fuertotes** y **sanotes** son muy viriles. Y el monitor es un verdadero Adonis.

Pepa   Sí, y seguro que es gay. Mira, chica, *déjate de tonterías* y ponte a **adelgazar** esos kilitos. Y en seguida verás cómo recuperas **el tipito**.

¿Lo has captado?

_____ 1. Pili is upset because she:
   a. has love handles
   b. doesn't fit into her clothes
   c. both *a* and *b*

_____ 2. When Pepa tells Pili that she's like a *foca*, this means she looks:
   a. pretty fat
   b. a little chubby
   c. very voluptuous

_____ 3. Although Pili has only gained five kilos, she seems much heavier because:
   a. it's all gone to her stomach
   b. her face is bloated
   c. she has a small frame

_____ 4. Pepa advises Pili to:
   a. go on a crash diet
   b. watch what she eats
   c. do a macrobiotic diet

_____ 5. During today's aerobics class, Pili:
   a. ran out of breath
   b. sweated a lot
   c. tore a muscle

_____ 6. After her first day at the gym, Pili feels really:
   a. exhausted
   b. reinvigorated
   c. out of shape

_____ 7. According to Pili, the gym is full of:
   a. hunky guys
   b. body builders
   c. gay men

Zooming in on health and fitness... We're going to focus on health and fitness since they've become a major obsession of modern life everywhere, and Spanish-speaking countries are no exception. And while we're on this topic, a little digression: since Latin cultures are very visual, people make certain comments in Spanish that would be virtually taboo in English. So don't fret if a friend remarks you're looking a little chubbier: it's a passing observation made in a spirit of affection and not intended to offend (though no one would say you look like **una foca** unless they really wanted to tease or prod you!). Likewise, if you're looking a little trimmer, you'll probably get eyed up and down and some appreciative remark will be made. And now back to where we left off . . . Ready? Get fit! Go!

¡Al grano!

adelgazar	to get thinner, to lose weight
apuntarse a (un gimnasio) [Spain]	to sign up at or join (a gym) ([syn] *matricularse or inscribirse*)
bajar de peso	to lose weight ([syn] *perder peso*)
el baño turco	the steam room
cachas [col, Spain]	hunky
la cinta [Spain]	the treadmill
engordar	to get fatter, to gain weight
en forma	fit; in shape (*estar en forma* = *to be fit*; *ponerse en forma* = *to get fit*)
(no) entrar en (la ropa)	to (not) fit into (one's clothes)
estar como una foca	to be really fat (*literally, to be like a seal*)
fuertote	robust, strong (*from fuerte*)
ganar peso	to gain weight ([syn] *subir de peso*)
la grasa	fat
hacer pesas	to lift weights, to do weight-lifting
hacer vida sana	to live healthily
los michelines [Spain]	love handles ([LA] *los rollos*)
pegar saltos	to jump up and down
pescado	fish (*as food, versus pez, which is the live animal*)
quitarse (el pan)	to cut out, to stop having (bread)
un régimen [Spain]	a diet ([syn] *una dieta; ponerse a régimen/dieta* = *to go on a diet*)
Sales como nuevo/a	You come out feeling new
sanote/a	robust, healthy (*from sano/a*)

ser de constitución (delgada/ fuerte)	to have a (small/large) build
sudar	to sweat
el tipito [Spain]	a good figure, a good body ([var] *un tipazo* = *a great body*)
la tripa [Spain]	belly
la verdurita	veggies (*diminutive of* **la verdura**)

¡Ojo!

Basta con (hacer un poco de ejercicio)	It's enough if you (do a little exercise)
como mucho	at most
como una bestia [col]	like crazy (*literally, like a beast*)
¡Déjate de tonterías!	Come on! Don't be ridiculous! Get serious!
una gozada [Spain]	great, fabulous, a real treat ([syn] *una delicia*)
meterse en (un sitio)	to go into (a place)
un montón (de toxinas) [col]	a lot (of toxins)
Se (te) nota	It shows; You can tell (*from* **notarse**, *which means "to show" or "to be obvious"*)
tipo (Schwarzenegger)	like (Schwarzenegger), the (Schwarzenegger) type

¡Te toca!

Replace the words in italics with one of the words or expressions below.

adelgazar	quitarme	cachas	apuntado a
régimen	engordar	se nota	como una foca

1. Desde que estoy a *dieta*, como muy poca grasa. _____

2. ¿Sabes qué? Ana se ha *hecho socia de* un gimnasio. _____

3. Juan hace pesas todos los días. Por eso está tan *fuertote*.

   _____

4. Va a ser difícil, pero he decidido *no tocar* el pan. _____

5. ¿Has visto a Luis últimamente? Se ha puesto *gordísimo*.

   _____

6. Quiero *perder* tres o cuatro kilos antes del verano. _____

7. Ese actor tuvo que *ganar* diez kilos para hacer la película.

   _____

8. *Se ve* que haces mucho ejercicio. Estás muy en forma. _____

Intercambio

Pili has canceled her *intercambio* with Tom this week. Meanwhile Tom and Pepa decide to go for a stroll. Fill in the blanks as you read their dialogue.

Pepa   Oye, Tom, te veo muy fuertote.

Tom   ¿Ah sí? ¿No estoy un poco gordo?

Pepa   Hombre, tienes un poco de tripa.

Tom   Sí, creo que he (1) _____ un par de kilos en México.

Pepa   No me extraña. Te pusiste loco con los tacos y tortillas.

Tom   Es que estaba todo buenísimo. Oye, ¿de verdad me ves gordo?

Pepa   Anda, ¡no te obsesiones! Se (2) _____ que tienes tripa, pero no pasa nada.

Tom   Pues casi no (3) _____ ya en mis pantalones.

Pepa   Vaya. Por cierto, ¿sabes que Pili se ha hecho socia de un gimnasio?

   ¿Por qué no te (4) _____ también?

Tom   Odio los gimnasios. Prefiero hacer ejercicio al aire libre.

Pepa   Bueno, si andas cinco o seis kilómetros al día,

   (5) _____ en seguida.

Tom   No es mala idea. A partir de mañana voy a andar una hora todos los días.

Pepa   Venga, te acompaño. Así me pongo en

   (6) _____ también.

Tom   Buena idea, que estás un poco fuertota también.

Pepa   ¿Me estás llamando gorda?

Tom   Gorda, no. ¡Estás como una (7) _____!

Pepa   ¡Venga ya!

Tom   Que no, tonta. Ya sabes que tienes un (8) _____

15

¡Nos vamos a poner moradas!

Pepa and Pili get ready to pig out

Pili Ya está, Pepa. Hoy rompo el régimen.

Pepa Pues venga, ¡**vamos a ponernos moradas**! ¿Has mirado **la carta**?

Pili *Estoy en ello*... Oye, **el menú del día** tiene una pinta estupenda.

Pepa Sí, me lo recomendó Juan y ya sabes que es *un obseso* de **la buena mesa**.

Pili Un obseso y un obeso. El tío está como una foca.

Pepa Sí, como muchos **sibaritas** *se pasa*. Y luego es **un goloso**...

Pili Por eso le gusta este sitio. Tienen **unos pasteles** muy **ricos**.

Pepa ¿Ah sí? ¡Qué peligro! En fin, ¿qué vas a tomar **de primero**?

Pili No sé. **Estoy dudando entre** el gazpacho y **los pimientos rellenos**.

Pepa Anda, pide los pimientos, y así **compartimos**.

Pili *No me fío*. Como eres **una tragona**, vas a acabar comiéndotelo todo.

Pepa Qué desagradable eres a veces. Dividimos **el plato** por la mitad, ¿vale?

Pili Bueno. ¿Tú qué vas a pedir **de primer plato**?

Pepa Los espárragos **a la plancha**, que son **de temporada**.

Pili Oye, Pepa, ¿y eso que están tomando en la mesa de al lado? Huele *de muerte*.

Pepa Es **un cocido madrileño**, creo.

Pili ¡Ah no!, **llena mucho**. Y desde lo de **las vacas locas** *me da un mal rollo* la carne...

Pepa Pero eso fue hace años, tonta. En todo caso, el cocido es casi todo **cerdo**.

Pili *Me da igual*. Es muy **pesado** y **me apetece** algo **ligero de segundo**. Así **me reservo** para el postre...

Pepa *Haces bien*, chica. ¡Ah!, mira, ahí viene el camarero.

¿Lo has captado?

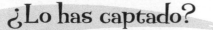

_____ 1. Pili remarks that the menu:
   a. looks pretty fancy
   b. has an appealing set-price lunch
   c. has a beautiful design

_____ 2. Pepa's friend Juan is really into:
   a. good food
   b. eating out
   c. cooking

_____ 3. Pili remarks that the cakes in the restaurant are really:
   a. rich
   b. delicious
   c. expensive

_____ 4. When Pili says Pepa is a *tragona*, this means she is:
   a. on the big side
   b. big on vegetables
   c. a big eater

_____ 5. Pepa is going to order the grilled asparagus because it's:
   a. healthy
   b. prepared in a delicious batter
   c. in season

_____ 6. The dish the people are having at the table beside them:
   a. smells great
   b. smells strange
   c. smells putrid

_____ 7. Pili doesn't want to order the *cocido* because:
   a. it has pork
   b. it's very filling
   c. she's not in the mood for it

_____ 8. Pili wants to have something light as a main course:
   a. to save room for dessert
   b. to not totally break her diet
   c. to avoid having indigestion

Zooming in on meals and eating out . . . Let's just say food is not something the Spanish take lightly. In fact, most Spaniards pride themselves on knowing the little bar just off the plaza that has the tastiest *tapas*, the place to go if you want a *real* paella, and the seafood restaurant where the fish was whisked in from the coast that morning. And then there's the infamous issue of mealtimes: nobody has lunch before two and dinner is usually around ten (though in Latin America mealtimes are usually a little earlier). What's more, meals are often major social occasions, and it's pretty standard for a Sunday lunch or a dinner out to last two or even three hours. Getting hunger pangs yet? Below you'll find some juicy vocabulary related to food and eating out.

¡Al grano!

a la plancha	grilled
la buena mesa	fine dining, good food
la carta	the menu
el cerdo	pork
el cocido madrileño	a stew made with chickpeas and pork (*typical in Madrid*)
compartir	to share
de primer plato *or* de primero	as a starter/appetizer/first course
de segundo plato *or* de segundo	as an entree/main course
de temporada [Spain]	in season
Estoy dudando entre *A* y *B*	I can't make up my mind between *A* and *B*
goloso/a (*adj and n*)	sweet-toothed (*ser goloso/a = to have a sweet tooth*)
ligero/a	light
Llena mucho	It's very filling
me apetece [Spain]	I feel like, I'm in the mood for ([LA] *se me antoja*)
el menú del día	luncheon special, set-price lunch
Me reservo para (el postre) [Spain]	I'm saving room for (dessert)
un pastel	a cake
pesado/a	heavy, rich (*for foods*)
pimientos rellenos	stuffed red peppers
un plato	a dish (*el primer/segundo plato = the first/second course*)
ponerse morado/a [col, Spain]	to pig out

el postre	dessert
rico/a	delicious
sibarita (*adj* and *n*)	gourmet, epicurean
Tiene buena pinta	It looks good ([var] *Tiene una pinta estupenda* = It looks great, see "First Impressions" later in this unit)
tragón/tragona (*adj* and *n*)	big eater, glutton
las vacas locas	mad cows, mad cow disease

¡Ojo!

de muerte [col]	fantastic, great
Estoy en ello	I'm working on it
Haces bien	Good idea; You're right (to do something)
Me da igual	It doesn't matter; I don't care
Me da (un) mal rollo [col, Spain]	It's a turn-off; It turns me off
No me fío	I don't trust (*you, it, him, her, etc.*)
un/a obseso/a (del jazz)	a (jazz) nut; big (on jazz)
pasarse	to overdo it, to go overboard

First Impressions

Tiene muy buena pinta

Pinta (literally, *paint*) is the informal equivalent of **aspecto** (*appearance*). So if something *tiene buena pinta* it means it has a good appearance, that is, it looks good. This expression is used a lot in reference to food, but it can also be used about people you don't know, movies you haven't seen, books you haven't read, or anything that you can't judge only by its physical appearance and that requires "sampling" (getting to know, tasting, watching, reading, listening, etc.). Here are a few examples:

Esa película tiene buena pinta.	That looks like a good movie.
Este libro no tiene mala pinta.	This book doesn't look bad.
El pescado tiene una pinta increíble.	The fish looks really incredible.

Ese hotelito tiene una pinta
  estupenda.

That looks like a great little
  hotel.

Ese tío tiene mala pinta.

That guy looks a bit shady.

Note that any adjective other than **bueno/a** or **malo/a** cannot go before **pinta**. In this case, put the article **una** before **pinta** and the adjective after.

¡Te toca!

Underline the word that best completes the sentence.

1. Hoy me **reservo** | **apetece** | **llena** tomar carne.

2. ¿Ponemos todo en el centro y lo **compartimos** | **dividimos** | **pasamos**?

3. —¿Qué vas a pedir?
   —No sé. Estoy **reservando** | **dudando** | **apeteciendo** entre la sopa y la ensalada.

4. Voy a pedir el menú del día. Tiene muy buena **pinta** | **carta** | **mesa**.

5. Mi amigo Jorge es muy **sibarita** | **tragón** | **goloso**. Le gusta mucho la buena mesa.

6. Como estoy a régimen, voy a tomar el pescado a la **carta** | **plancha** | **dieta**.

7. La verdura siempre es más rica cuando es de **sibarita** | **plancha** | **temporada**.

8. Este pastel de chocolate **huele** | **llena** | **duda** mucho.

Intercambio

Pili has canceled her *intercambio* with Tom again this week. Meanwhile, Tom and Pepa decide to go out for lunch at a local restaurant. Fill in the blanks as you read their dialogue.

Tom   ¿Has mirado la carta ya?

Pepa   Un momento. Estoy (1) _____

_____ .

Tom   No tardes mucho por favor. Tengo un hambre que me muero.

Pepa   Vale, vale. Pero es que todo tiene muy buena (2) _____.

Tom   Sí, y encima es barato. Te recomendó Juan este sitio, ¿verdad?

Pepa   Sí, y ya sabes lo sibarita que es.

Tom   Es verdad, le gusta mucho la (3) _____ _____.

Pepa   Bueno, ¿has decidido lo que vas a tomar de primer

(4) _____?

Tom   Pues estoy (5) _____ entre la paella y la sopa
de pescado.

Pepa   ¿Y si pedimos varios platos y los compartimos?

Tom   Buena idea. Me (6) _____ más eso que tomar
un menú del día.

Pepa   Sí, así probamos un poco de todo.

Tom   Pues prepárate, Pepa, que ¡nos vamos a poner (7) _____!

16

El quinto pino

Pili looks for a new place

Pepa   Oye, Pili, ¿qué tal el **piso** que has visto hoy?

Pili   **Un cuchitril**. Oscuro, pequeño, **dando a un patio interior**. Y encima caro.

Pepa   Vaya. Pues dicen que **los alquileres** han subido mucho últimamente. A lo mejor no es el momento para buscar casa.

Pili   Mira, Pepa, *no tengo más remedio*. **Mi casero** ya ha vendido **la casa** donde estoy, y tengo un mes para encontrar algo.

Pepa   Pues *ponte las pilas*, chica. ¿No has visto nada que te guste?

Pili   Sí, **un ático** por La Latina, pero claro, estaba **fuera de mi presupuesto**.

Pepa   Tranquila, ya encontrarás algún chollo. ¿Eso es el *Segunda Mano* de hoy?

Pili   Sí. ¿Le *echamos un vistazo*?

Pepa   Venga. A ver, pisos en alquiler, de 400 a 600 euros. ¡Ah!, mira esto, **buhardilla**, **céntrica**, **amueblada**, **cocina americana**, muy **coqueta**.

Pili   Pepa, ¿sabes lo que es **un último piso** en verano? ¡Te asfixias! Y en invierno te mueres de frío. Mira, tía, *ni muerta*...

Pepa   Vale, vale. ¿Y éste? **Apartamento** en **edificio reformado**, **exterior**, **calefacción central**, **ascensor**, **balcón a la calle**, muy **luminoso**.

Pili   Ah, *no suena mal*. ¿Está por **el centro**?

Pepa   No, en Aluche. Pero no está mal esa zona. Y está **bien comunicada**.

Pili   ¡Qué dices! Es **el quinto pino**, Pepa. ¡*Ni loca* me voy a vivir allí!

Pepa   Bueno, vale. Espera, ahora que lo pienso, **mi vecina se traslada** a Vigo el mes que viene. Y creo que su apartamento va a quedar *libre*.

Pili   ¿Ah sí? Pues tu **barrio** me encanta. Venga, vamos a llamarla corriendo...

¿Lo has captado?

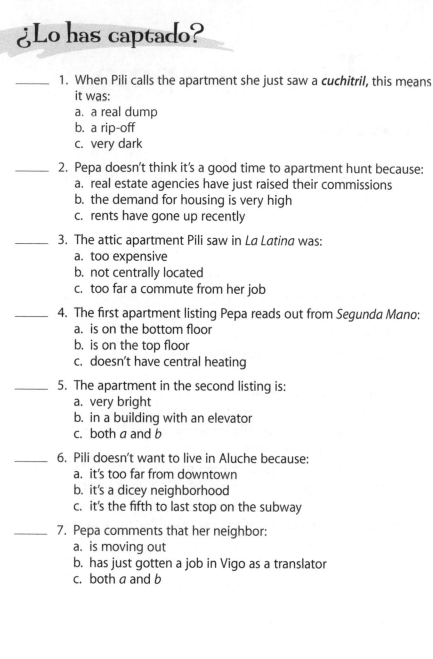

_____ 1. When Pili calls the apartment she just saw a *cuchitril,* this means it was:
   a. a real dump
   b. a rip-off
   c. very dark

_____ 2. Pepa doesn't think it's a good time to apartment hunt because:
   a. real estate agencies have just raised their commissions
   b. the demand for housing is very high
   c. rents have gone up recently

_____ 3. The attic apartment Pili saw in *La Latina* was:
   a. too expensive
   b. not centrally located
   c. too far a commute from her job

_____ 4. The first apartment listing Pepa reads out from *Segunda Mano*:
   a. is on the bottom floor
   b. is on the top floor
   c. doesn't have central heating

_____ 5. The apartment in the second listing is:
   a. very bright
   b. in a building with an elevator
   c. both *a* and *b*

_____ 6. Pili doesn't want to live in Aluche because:
   a. it's too far from downtown
   b. it's a dicey neighborhood
   c. it's the fifth to last stop on the subway

_____ 7. Pepa comments that her neighbor:
   a. is moving out
   b. has just gotten a job in Vigo as a translator
   c. both *a* and *b*

Zooming in on housing . . . Frankly, it's a mystery how *Mi casa es tu casa* ever became an expression. In Spain (though not in Latin America) *mi casa* is definitely not *tu casa*, and if you do get invited to a Spaniard's house, consider it a great honor. Also, don't even *think* of dropping in on someone if you're in the neighborhood: it's tantamount to an act of invasion! This is because the Spanish do most of their socializing in public places, and one's home is a sanctuary in which to rest and refuel. Still, this doesn't mean people don't talk about their lairs. And who knows? You might decide to live in a Spanish-speaking country for a while and find yourself doing a little apartment hunting. In any event, you'll need some vocabulary to talk about where you hang your hat.

¡Al grano!

un alquiler	a rent, a rental (*en alquiler* = *for rent*)
amueblado/a	furnished (*sin amueblar* = *unfurnished*)
un apartamento [Spain]	a one-bedroom apartment; [LA] an apartment (*Note that in some Latin American countries,* **departamento** *is more common.*)
un ascensor	an elevator
un ático	a penthouse apartment, usually with a terrace
un balcón	a balcony (*un balcón a la calle is a balcony facing onto the street*)
un barrio	a neighborhood
bien comunicado/a [Spain]	with good public transportation
una buhardilla [Spain]	a small attic apartment
calefacción central	central heating
una casa	a house (*Note that* **casa** *is also used to refer to the place where one lives, whether this is a house or an apartment. Therefore* **la casa de María** = *Maria's place and* **en casa** = *at home.*)
el casero/la casera	the landlord/landlady
céntrico/a	centrally located
el centro	the center, downtown
una cocina americana	a kitchenette
coqueto/a [Spain]	cute, charming
un cuchitril	a rat hole, a dump
dar a	to face onto
un edificio	a building

exterior [Spain]	outward-facing (*facing onto the street*)
fuera del presupuesto	not in the budget, beyond the budget
interior [Spain]	inward-facing (*facing onto an inner courtyard or shaft*)
luminoso/a	bright, with lots of light
un patio	a courtyard
un piso [Spain]	an apartment with two or more bedrooms
el (último) piso	the (top) floor
el quinto pino [Spain]	very far away, out in the boondocks (*literally, the fifth pine*)
reformado/a	renovated
trasladarse (de casa) [Spain]	to move (house) ([syn] *mudarse*)
un/a vecino/a	a neighbor

¡Ojo!

echar un vistazo	to take a look
libre	available, free (*versus **gratis**, which means free of charge*)
¡Ni loco/a!	No way; Not even if I were crazy
¡Ni muerto/a!	No way (*literally, Not even if I were dead*)
No suena mal	It doesn't sound bad
No tengo más remedio	I don't have a choice; I've got no other option
ponerse las pilas [col]	to get moving; to get on the job (*literally, to put in one's batteries*)

¡Te toca!

You phone to get more information about an apartment you saw listed in the paper. Circle the correct words in the conversation you have with the owner.

Tú   Buenos días. Llamo por el apartamento que está en alquiler.

Casera   ¡Ah sí! Pues le cuento. Es un tercer (1) **piso** | **apartamento** | **planta**, exterior, con dos (2) **balcones** | **patios** | **vigas** a la calle.

Tú   ¡Ah!, entonces será muy (3) **brillante** | **luminoso** | **luz**.

Casera   Bueno, luz directa no tiene porque (4) **comunica** | **da** | **pone** al norte. Pero claro, tampoco es oscuro. Y es muy fresquito en verano.

Tú   ¿Y tiene (5) **calefacción** | **calentando** | **calentamiento** central?

Casera   Sí, y el (6) **cuchitril | piso | edificio** es nuevo y tiene ascensor. En fin, es un apartamentito muy coqueto. Ideal para una persona.

Tú   Ajá. Por cierto, ¿en qué zona está?

Casera   En el Barrio de la Concepción. ¿Lo conoce?

Tú   No. ¿Eso está por el (7) **quinto pino | centro | exterior**?

Casera   No, pero está muy bien (8) **conectado | comunicado | trasladado**. Tiene metro y varios autobuses.

Tú   Pues muchas gracias, pero la verdad es que busco algo más (9) **céntrico | interior | amueblado**.

Intercambio

A week later, Pili has settled into her new place and invites Tom over. Fill in the blanks as you read their dialogue.

Pili   Entra, entra. Te enseño mi nueva casa.

Tom   ¡Ah, qué bonita! Y tienes mucha luz.

Pili   Sí, el salón es muy (1) _____ _____. Entra luz todo el día.

Tom   Claro, es que esa ventana (2) _____ al sur, ¿no?

Pili   Sí, y aquélla al este. En fin, el dormitorio es más oscuro como

es (3) _____.

Tom   Mejor. Si fuese exterior, oirías todo el ruido de la calle.

Pili   Tienes razón. Además este (4) ___ _____ tiene mucha marcha por la noche.

Tom   También tiene unos restaurantes muy buenos. Hay un italiano cerca donde se come muy bien.

Pili   ¡Ah! Entonces, ¿ya conocías la zona?

Tom   Claro. Mi novia es (5) _____ tuya.

Pili   Pero, ¡qué tonta soy! Es verdad, Pepa vive aquí al lado.

Tom   Y fue gracias a ella que encontraste esto, ¿no?

Pili   Bueno, sí. Pero, ¿te lo puedes creer? Me quiso mandar a vivir a Aluche.

Tom   ¿Ah sí? Un compañero mío del trabajo se (6) _____ allí

        hace poco. Y me dijo que estaba muy bien (7) _____.

Pili   Eso dicen. Pero mira, Tom, entre tú y yo, es el (8) _____

        _____

17

Un poco pachucha

Pili's a little under the weather

Pili   ¿Sí?

Pepa   Soy yo, Pepa. ¿**Se te ha pasado** el resfriado?

Pili   ¡Qué dices! Me quiero morir. De verdad, **me encuentro** fatal.

Pepa   Yo también estoy un poco **pachucha**. Será un virus *que anda por ahí*.

Pili   Espera, *no cuelgues*, me tengo que **sonar**...

(unos segundos después)

Pepa   Pues **estás hecha una pena**, hija.

Pili   *Calla*, que aparte de **los mocos**, la garganta **me duele** *que no veas*. ¿Te lo puedes creer?, **me cuesta** hasta tragar líquido.

Pepa   Nada, tienes un **catarrazo**. En fin, **es la época**. Todo el mundo **está constipado**.

Pili   Oye, guapa, esto no es **un constipado**. Anoche **me dio un bajón** que casi me **desmayo**. Te lo juro, estuve a punto de irme a **urgencias**.

Pepa   Bueno, pero tú **te mareas** fácilmente. Como tienes **la tensión baja**...

Pili   No eres ningún consuelo, tía. Eres como **mi médico de cabecera** que ayer en **la consulta** me dijo que lo mío no era nada **grave**. Fíjate, *el muy cerdo se negó a* darme **la baja**.

Pepa   Claro, se habrá dado cuenta de que eres una hipocondríaca tremenda. En fin, ¿no te **recetó** nada?

Pili   Sí, **unas pastillas** y **un jarabe para la tos**. Y hasta ahora no han tenido ningún efecto. Mira, Pepa, lo que tengo es **un gripazo** y *no hay tu tía*. Aparte de que hablar contigo me está dando **dolor de cabeza**.

Pepa   Oye, no te pongas *borde*. ¿Quieres que te haga una visita y te lleve un par de revistas?

Pili   ¡Ah sí! Anda, compra el último *Hola*, que eso sí que será terapéutico.

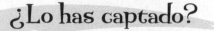

¿Lo has captado?

_____ 1. Pepa and Pili are chatting:
    a. on the phone
    b. through the intercom of Pili's building
    c. on the Internet

_____ 2. When Pepa says she's a little **pachucha**, this means she:
    a. has a bad cold
    b. feels a little under the weather
    c. has hay fever

_____ 3. Pili asks Pepa to hold on while she:
    a. gargles
    b. sneezes
    c. blows her nose

_____ 4. Pepa claims that everybody:
    a. has a stomach virus now
    b. is constipated now
    c. has a cold now

_____ 5. Pili tells Pepa that the night before she:
    a. had a really high fever
    b. almost passed out
    c. was in a cold sweat

_____ 6. Pili is upset with her doctor because he:
    a. gave her the wrong prescription
    b. refused to give her sick leave
    c. told her she was a hypochondriac

_____ 7. Pili claims that she has:
    a. a nasty flu
    b. a terrible cold
    c. horrible intestinal pain

Zooming in on sickness and pain . . . Brace yourselves, ye faint of heart! The Spanish aren't at all squeamish or discreet about sickness and pain (although Latin Americans are a little more discreet). In fact, they occupy as honored a spot in the daily repertoire as the weather. OK, this is partly because bodily functions and malfunctions aren't considered distasteful or taboo in Spain. But it's also because the Spanish love talking, and one's physical state is a great standby topic. So be warned: your *amigos* will be direct on this front, whether it's a comment casually tossed off about the horrors of menstruation, constipation, or irritable bowel syndrome, or an in-depth account of their latest physical ailments. Meanwhile, here's some vocabulary to wield when you're not feeling in top form.

¡Al grano!

la baja [Spain]	sick leave (*estar de baja = to be on sick leave*)
un bajón	a sharp drop in blood pressure (*in other contexts, this could be a general turn for the worse or a downward mood swing, like a depression*)
un catarro	a cold ([var] *un catarrazo = a bad cold*)
un constipado	a cold (*tener un constipado or estar constipado/a = to have a cold; estar estreñido/a = to be constipated*)
la consulta *or* **el consultorio**	the clinic, the doctor's office
costar	to require an effort (*Me cuesta tragar = It's hard for me to swallow*)
dar	to get (*for symptoms; Me da alergia en primavera = I get hay fever in the spring*)
desmayarse	to pass out, to faint
un dolor de (cabeza/muelas/ espalda...)	a (head/tooth/back) ache
encontrarse	to feel ([syn] *sentirse*)
Es la época	It's that time of year
estar hecho/a una pena [Spain]	to be a wreck
grave	serious
la gripe	the flu ([var] *un gripazo = a nasty flu*)
un jarabe	a syrup (*un jarabe para la tos = cough syrup*)
marearse	to feel faint, to get dizzy

Me duele (la garganta)	(my throat) hurts (*from doler, which means to hurt or to ache*)
un médico de cabecera	a general practitioner, a family doctor
los mocos	mucus (*Tengo muchos mocos* = *I have a runny nose*)
pachucho/a [Spain]	under the weather
una pastilla	a pill or tablet
que anda por ahí	that's going around
recetar	to prescribe
¿Se te ha pasado...?	Have you gotten over . . . ?
sonarse (la nariz)	to blow one's nose
la tensión	blood pressure ([LA] *la presión*)
la tos	cough, coughing
urgencias	the emergency room

¡Ojo!

borde [col, Spain]	rude, nasty (*No te pongas borde* = *Don't get nasty*)
el muy cerdo	the total pig, the total bastard (**Muy** *can be inserted this way for emphasis with all the words listed in "Poking Fun and Insulting" in Unit 3.*)
Calla [col, Spain]	Don't remind me; I know (*strong slang; literally, be quiet*)
No cuelgues	Hold on (*for the telephone; literally, Don't hang up*)
negarse (a hacer algo)	to refuse (to do something)
que no veas [col, Spain]	like you wouldn't believe, a lot
y no hay tu tía [Spain]	and that's that; and there's no getting around it

¡Te toca!

Complete the dialogue between Pili and her family doctor by underlining the correct word.

Médico   ¿En qué le puedo ayudar?

Pili   Pues me (1) **estoy** | **encuentro** | **duele** muy mal. Creo que tengo la (2) **virus** | **gripe** | **baja**.

Médico   Vamos a ver. ¿Tiene fiebre?

Pili   No, pero me (3) **sueno** | **mareo** | **duelo** mucho.

Médico   Será que tiene la tensión un poco baja. ¿Qué otros síntomas tiene?

Pili   Pues me (4) **cuesta** | **duele** | **da** muchísimo la garganta. Bueno, y también tengo muchos (5) **mocos** | **tos** | **resfriados**. Estoy todo el rato sonándome.

Médico   No se preocupe. Lo que tiene es un resfriado común. En fin, es normal en esta época.

Pili   ¿Ah sí? Bueno, pero no puedo ir al trabajo en este estado...

Médico   Claro que puede, mujer. Si hoy es sábado. Ya verá como se le (6) **da** | **pasa** | **anda** esto antes del lunes.

Pili   ¿Entonces no me va a dar la (7) **baja** | **pastilla** | **receta**?

Médico   No, pero le voy a (8) **tomar** | **recetar** | **sonar** unas pastillas y un jarabe para la tos. Tómelos tres veces al día y se encontrará mejor en seguida.

Intercambio

It's Sunday morning and Pili has canceled her *intercambio* with Tom since she still isn't feeling well. Meanwhile Tom and Pepa laze around having breakfast and reading the Sunday paper. Fill in the blanks as you read their dialogue.

Tom   ¿Estás bien?, Pepa. Te veo muy pálida.

Pepa   ¿Ah sí? Pues la verdad es que me (1) _____ fatal.

Tom   ¿Qué te pasa? ¿Tienes (2) _____ de cabeza?

Pepa   No, estoy (3) _____, creo.

Tom   ¡Qué asco! Por favor no me cuentes más.

Pepa   Pero ¿qué ocurre? Es una cosa muy normal...

Tom   Ya lo sé. Pero mira, Pepa, en Estados Unidos somos un poco más discretos.

Pepa   ¿Ah sí? ¿No habláis nunca de los mocos?

Tom   ¿Los mocos? Ah, perdón. Te entendí mal.

Pepa   Anda, pásame un Kleenex que me tengo

que (4) _____ otra vez.

Tom   Toma. Por cierto, tienes una tos horrible.

Pepa   Ya lo sé. En fin, estoy hecha una (5) _____.

Tom   Oye, ¿quieres que vaya a la farmacia a comprarte unas

         (6) _____?

Pepa   Es domingo, Tom. Están todas cerradas.

Tom   Es verdad. Pues vete a la (7) _____ mañana, a ver
         lo que te dice el médico.

Pepa   No, ya se me pasará.

Tom   Pues ahora que lo dices a mí también (8) _____ _____
         la garganta.

Pepa   ¿Ah sí? Entonces estamos los dos un poco pachuchos...

18

Es una víbora...

Pepa and Pili gossip about celebrities and friends

Pepa   ¡Qué hombre más **hortera**! *Fíjate* el abrigo de piel que lleva.

Pili   Bueno, es un poco **extravagante** pero *me hace gracia*. Además dicen que es un tío muy **progre**.

Pepa   También he oído que es **un egoísta** tremendo y que **tiene un genio**...

Pili   *Normal*, como todos los artistas. Mira, no me vas a *cambiar de idea*. A mí me cae genial ese tío. Aparte de que **está buenísimo**.

Pepa   ¿Lo ves atractivo? En fin, chica, *sobre gustos no hay nada escrito*.

Pili   La que me *da repelús* es su mujer. Es **una víbora**...

Pepa   Pues es una tía muy **culta** y **preparada**. *Por lo visto* vale mucho.

Pili   ¡Qué dices! Ésa es **una interesada** y encima va de **diva**...

Pepa   Nada, **le tienes manía** porque está con ése. Bueno, dejemos de mirar el *Hola* y hablemos de tu fiesta. A ver, ¿a quién vas a invitar?

Pili   No sé, va a ser difícil. En mi nueva casa caben como mucho treinta personas.

Pepa   Pues venga, hacemos la lista. Paco, Teresa, Mónica, Manolo, Pedro, Ana...

Pili   Ana no, que es una aguafiestas. Yo sólo quiero gente **divertida**.

Pepa   Bueno, es un poco seria pero es **simpática**. Por lo menos a mí me parece **maja**.

Pili   ¿Ah sí? Pues cuando bebe se pone super borde la tía. Es muy **desagradable**.

Pepa   Bueno, vale, Ana no. ¿Y José Luis? Ése sí que es muy **gracioso** y **vital**.

Pili   Sí, es un tío **encantador**. Y muy **listo**. Pero su novia es más **rara**...

Pepa   Tienes razón. *De entrada* es muy **dulce** y **educada**, pero luego es **una envidiosa**. Y **tiene una mala leche**...

Pili   Sí, es un poco **bruja**. En fin, él tampoco es un santo. Venga, *apúntalos* en la lista, que **animarán** *el tema*. En una fiesta *hace falta* un poco de **emoción**...

¿Lo has captado?

_____ 1. At the beginning Pepa and Pili are:
  a. looking at snapshots
  b. people-watching at a café
  c. leafing through a gossip magazine

_____ 2. Pepa thinks the way the guy dresses is:
  a. overly extravagant
  b. really tacky
  c. effeminate

_____ 3. Pepa adds that the guy is egotistical and:
  a. has a bad temper
  b. thinks he's hot
  c. acts like he's a genius

_____ 4. Pili likes the guy and thinks he's:
  a. a really good person
  b. very sexy
  c. a great artist

_____ 5. When Pili says the guy's wife is _una interesada_, this means she's:
  a. an interesting person
  b. a curious person
  c. out for herself

_____ 6. When Pepa says the guy's wife is _culta_, this means she's:
  a. a member of a cult
  b. cultured
  c. a culture vulture

_____ 7. According to Pili, when Ana drinks, she gets really:
  a. raucous
  b. depressed
  c. out of line

_____ 8. At first Jose Luis' girlfriend seems very sweet and:
  a. educated
  b. polite
  c. friendly

_____ 9. Pili thinks parties should be:
  a. lively and exciting
  b. emotionally charged
  c. small and intimate

Zooming in on personality . . . Yes, Latins love to gossip. And in Spain, talking about people is a national hobby that's more popular than flamenco and bullfighting put together. But before you break down and buy *Hola* magazine to get the latest on royalty, local celebrities, and Hollywood stars, be warned. This terrain is rife with false cognates—that is, words that are similar in Spanish and English but have different meanings. For example, *una persona extravagante* does not splurge, *una persona educada* might be illiterate, and *una persona interesada* may have no interests at all. Nor is *gracioso gracious*, *simpático sympathetic*, or *teniendo genio having a streak of genius*. Enough said. Below you'll find a list of key adjectives and expressions related to personality.

¡Al grano!

Adjectives

bueno/a	sexy, "hot" (*when used with estar and referring to people*)
culto/a	knowledgeable, educated, well read
divertido/a	fun
dulce	gentle, sweet, kind
educado/a	polite, well-mannered
encantador/a	wonderful, great, charming
extravagante	eccentric, flamboyant
egoísta*	selfish, egotistical
envidioso/a*	envious
gracioso/a*	funny, witty
hortera* [Spain]	tacky, in bad taste
interesado/a*	self-seeking, out for himself/herself
listo/a*	clever, smart
majo/a [Spain]	nice
preparado/a	competent, able
progre* [col]	liberal
raro/a	strange, weird
simpático/a	friendly, nice
vital	high-energy, full of life

*These adjectives, which are generally negative, are often used as nouns for added emphasis. When this is done with some positive adjectives, they take a negative meaning (Un listo = a smart aleck).

Nouns and expressions

animar (la fiesta)	to liven up (the party)
una bruja	a witch
una diva	a prima donna (*va de diva* = *she acts like she's a prima donna*)
Me hace gracia	I find him/her amusing or appealing; I like him/her
Sobre gustos no hay nada escrito	There's no accounting for taste
tener (mal) genio	to have a (bad) temper
tener mala leche [col, Spain]	to be nasty or vindictive, to have a mean streak (*literally, to have bad milk*)
tener manía (a alguien) [Spain]	to dislike (somebody)
Vale mucho	S/he has really wonderful qualities; S/he's really talented (*In this context it means "She's really good at what she does"*)
una víbora	a person with a vicious tongue (*literally, a viper*)

¡Ojo!

apuntar	to write down
cambiar de idea	to change one's mind
dar repelús	to give the creeps
de entrada	at first, at the beginning
emoción	excitement
Fíjate...	Get a load of . . . ; Just look at . . . (*from fijarse, which means to notice or to observe*)
Hace falta	One needs; We need
Normal [Spain]	Of course; Naturally
por lo visto	apparently
el tema [col, Spain]	things, the "thing"

¡Te toca!

How would you describe the following people? Match the sentences on the left with a description on the right.

_____ 1. He has a very short fuse. a. **Es graciosísimo.**

_____ 2. She's a lot of fun. b. **Es un interesado.**

_____ 3. He cracks me up. c. **Es muy vital.**

_____ 4. She's very polite. d. **Es cultísima.**

_____ 5. He's just out for himself. e. **Tiene mucho genio.**

_____ 6. She's got a lot of energy. f. **Es super listo.**

_____ 7. He's really smart. g. **Es bastante borde.**

_____ 8. He can be pretty rude. h. **Es muy educada.**

_____ 9. She's very well-read. i. **Está buenísima.**

_____ 10. She's a real fox. j. **Es muy divertida.**

Intercambio

The day after Pili's party, Tom and Pili meet up for their *intercambio.*
Fill in the blanks as you read their dialogue.

Pili ¿Lo pasaste bien anoche?

Tom Sí, genial. Y tus amigos son muy (1) _____.

Pili Sí, tú también les caíste bien. Bueno, estuviste mucho tiempo
hablando con José Luis, ¿no?

Tom Sí. Me pareció un hombre muy <u>educado</u>.

Pili ¿José Luis? De educado nada... De hecho puede

ser muy (2) _____.

Tom Ah, perdón, me confundí. Quería decir que es una
persona que lee mucho. Sabe mucho de historia
y filosofía.

Pili Eso sí. Es muy (3) _____. ¿Y hablaste
con su novia?

Tom Muy poco. Pero parece buena persona.

Pili   ¡Ja! ¡Es una bruja! Envidiosa, egoísta y tiene una mala

(4) _____...

Tom   Veo que no te cae nada bien.

Pili   Sí, le tengo un poco de (5) ___ _____. ¿Y hablaste con mi amiga Mónica?

Tom   Ah sí, me reí mucho con ella. Es muy (6) _____.

Pili   Sí, Mónica es la monda.

Tom   ¿Y quién era ése que iba vestido como Elvis Presley?

Pili   ¡Ah!, Manolo... Es un poco (7) _____ pero es muy majo.

Tom   Sí, me hizo mucha (8) _____. En fin, Pili, tienes unos amigos encantadores...

19

Los domingueros

Pepa and Pili do a little hiking

Pepa   ¿Subimos ese **cerro**?

Pili   ¡Estás loca! Está lleno de **matorrales** y no hay ningún **sendero**.

Pepa   *¿Qué más da?* Vamos **campo a través**. Más divertido...

Pili   ¡Que no!, Pepa. Tiene mucha **pendiente. Tardaríamos** un par de horas en llegar **hasta arriba**.

Pepa   ¿Pero no querías darte una buena **caminata**?

Pili   Sí, pero con tanta **cuesta arriba** no. Además, ya es la una y *me está entrando un hambre*...

Pepa   ¡Anda ya! Eres como **los domingueros** que se van a **la sierra, dan un paseo** de media hora y ¡*hala!*, a comer.

Pili   Pues sinceramente no me parece mala idea parar en algún sitio a tomar algo...

Pepa   Pero ¿no llevas comida en **la mochila**?

Pili   Sí, pero una cervecita fría no.

Pepa   ¡Venga ya! No seas pesada, y disfruta un poco del campo.

Pili   Tienes razón. La verdad es que *da gusto* respirar este **aire puro** del **monte**.

Pepa   *Ya te digo.* Sobre todo después de la **contaminación** de Madrid.

Pili   Pues me encantaría montar **una casa rural**, ¿sabes? En un lugar **retirado** donde se puedan **practicar deportes al aire libre**.

Pepa   ¡Pero si eres totalmente urbana! *Te morirías del asco* después de dos días.

Pili   Ya veo que no conoces mi lado **campestre**... Oye, Pepa, esto es **privado**, ¿no?

Pepa   Sí, acabo de ver **un cartel** que ponía **coto de caza**.

Pili   Será **la finca** de al lado. Aquí hay **toros bravos**, tía.

Pepa   ¡No me digas!

Pili   *Lo que oyes.* ¿No ves ése detrás de aquel árbol? Venga, corre...

¿Lo has captado?

_____ 1. Pili doesn't want to climb the hill because it's:
   a. very craggy
   b. full of wild goats
   c. covered in brush

_____ 2. Pili also doesn't want to climb the hill because:
   a. it's very steep
   b. she's getting hungry
   c. both *a* and *b*

_____ 3. Pepa accuses Pili of being lazy by comparing her to:
   a. a Dominican priest
   b. a Sunday day-tripper
   c. a person from Santo Domingo

_____ 4. Pili comments that the mountain air is:
   a. a bit gusty
   b. clean
   c. very nippy

_____ 5. Pepa is happy to get out of Madrid because of the:
   a. pollution
   b. litter
   c. crowds

_____ 6. Pili says she'd like to:
   a. live in the country when she retires
   b. run a rural bed and breakfast
   c. take up an outdoor sport

_____ 7. Pepa thinks they've wandered into:
   a. private hunting grounds
   b. a cattle ranch
   c. a wildlife reserve

_____ 8. At the end, Pepa and Pili start running because they:
   a. are on private property
   b. want to get some exercise
   c. see a wild bull

Zooming in on nature and the outdoors . . . Of course this is a huge topic, and you'd need an encyclopedia if you wanted to know all the names of plants, trees, and land features. Here we're just going to deal with some of the more common words and expressions regarding nature and the outdoors, as well as one of the most popular weekend activities in Spain: walking in the country. In fact, the *dominguero* is a national phenomenon, and roads are jammed on Sunday mornings as hoards of urbanites head off to the nearby mountains or their relatives' villages. Typical Sunday outings involve a little stroll followed by a big lunch (or vice versa), though serious hiking is also popular in Spain.

¡Al grano!

al aire libre	outdoors (*deportes al aire libre* = *outdoor sports; see "Outdoor Exercise" later in this unit*)
el aire puro	clean air
una caminata [Spain]	a long walk; a hike (*darse una caminata* = *to go on a hike*)
campestre	country, rural
campo a través	cross-country
un cartel	a sign
una casa rural [Spain]	a rural bed and breakfast
un cerro	a hill ([syn] *una colina*)
la contaminación	pollution
un coto de caza [Spain]	private hunting grounds
cuesta arriba/abajo [Spain]	uphill/downhill
dar un paseo	to go for a stroll
un/a dominguero/a [Spain]	a Sunday excursionist (*a city dweller who goes off to the country on Sunday*)
una finca	a ranch, an estate
hasta arriba	to the top
un matorral	brush, thicket, scrub
una mochila	a backpack
el monte	the mountain
una pendiente	a slope, an incline (*Tiene mucha pendiente* = *It's very steep*)
practicar *or* hacer deportes	to do sports
privado	private (property)
retirado/a	off the beaten track
un sendero	a path, a trail ([syn] *un camino*)

la sierra	the mountains (*but una sierra = a mountain range*)
tarda (una hora)	it takes (an hour) (*Tardaríamos una hora means "it would take us an hour"*)
un toro bravo	a fighting bull (*a bull bred for bullfighting*)

¡Ojo!

Da gusto (respirar)	It feels great (to breathe . . .)
¡Hala!	Whoa! My goodness! (*interjection used to express surprise*)
Lo que oyes [col]	I'm not kidding; Seriously
Me está entrando hambre/ sed/sueño [Spain]	I'm getting really hungry/thirsty/tired ([LA] *Me está dando hambre/sed/sueño*)
morirse del asco [col, Spain]	to not be able to take/stand something (*literally, to die of disgust*)
¿Qué más da?	So what? Who cares?
Ya te digo [col, Spain]	You said it! You're telling me! (*when used informally*)

Outdoor Exercise

¿Practicas algún deporte al aire libre?

Note that *practicar* here is not *practice* but *do*, though it's also common to use *hacer* with sports. Meanwhile, for you fresh air nuts, below is a list of common outdoor sports:

bucear	to scuba dive
escalar	to mountain-climb
esquiar	to ski
hacer footing	to jog
hacer/practicar senderismo	to trek or hike
hacer surf/windsurf	to surf/windsurf
hacer vela	to sail
montar en bici	to cycle
montar a caballo	to ride horseback
pescar	to fish

¡Te toca!

Underline the word that best completes the sentence.

1. Vamos a darnos un **paseo** | **camino** | **sendero**. Me apetece andar un poco.

2. Este camino tiene mucha **colina** | **pendiente** | **matorral**.

3. A Lola le gustan mucho los deportes al aire **fresco** | **libre** | **puro**.

4. Los fines de semana este pueblo se llena de **retirados** | **senderos** | **domingueros**.

5. ¿Hacemos una excursión a **los montes** | **las montañas** | **la sierra** mañana?

6. Estoy cansadísima. Nos hemos dado **un camino** | **una pendiente** | **una caminata** muy fuerte.

7. ¿Cuánto se **tarda** | **toma** | **lleva** andando desde El Escorial a Peralejo?

8. ¡Estás loco! ¿De verdad quieres **montar** | **subir** | **cuesta arriba** aquel monte?

Intercambio

This time Tom has canceled his *intercambio* with Pili to go hiking in the mountains with Pepa. Fill in the blanks in the dialogue below.

Pepa   ¡Qué bien salir de la ciudad y respirar un poco de aire

       (1) _____!

Tom   Sí, ha sido una buena idea venir a la sierra hoy.

Pepa   Oye, ¿llevas agua en la (2) _____?

Tom   Sí, ¿quieres un poco?

Pepa   Ahora no, pero nos va a (3) _____ sed más adelante. Ese monte es todo cuesta arriba.

Tom   Pero, ¿vamos a (4) _____ ese monte?

Pepa   Claro. ¿No te querías dar una buena caminata?

Tom   Sí, pero no hay ningún (5) _____.

Pepa   Hay uno más arriba. Pero aquí abajo tenemos

       que ir campo (6) _____ _____.

Tom   ¿Y viniste aquí con Pili la semana pasada?

Pepa Sí, pero al final sólo nos dimos un (7) _____ de media hora.

Tom   ¿Por qué?

Pepa Bueno, entramos sin querer en una (8) _____ de toros bravos.

Tom   ¿Sí? ¿Y qué hicisteis?

Pepa Nada, salimos de allí corriendo. Y luego nos pusimos moradas como buenos domingueros.

Un chiringuito con encanto

Pepa and Pili get into beach mode

Pepa   *Esto es vida*. Sentada aquí, mirando al horizonte.

Pili   Yo no miro tan lejos. Ese **surfista** que acaba de entrar está buenísimo.

Pepa   Un poquito joven para ti, ¿no? Tendrá como mucho veinte años.

Pili   *¿Y qué?* Es alto y guapo. Y ese *aire* **playero** me mata.

Pepa   Pues *dedícate al* surf, chica. Ya tienes un motivo.

Pili   *Olvídate*, odio **las olas**. Me gusta el mar cuando está **como un plato**.

Pepa   Entonces lo tienes *crudo*. Por cierto, **te has quemado** un poco.

Pili   Sí, se me olvidó ponerme **crema** esta mañana.

Pepa   ¡Estás loca! **Hacía un sol de justicia** en esa calita.

Pili   Sí, **pegaba fuerte**. Pero bueno, ese **chapuzón** me **refrescó** bastante.

Pepa   Pero si te **metiste** un momento y **saliste** corriendo...

Pili   Suficiente. No necesito **darme un baño** de media hora como tú. Oye, seguro que fuiste **pez** en una vida anterior.

Pepa   Y tú **lagarto**, guapa. Tal como **tomas el sol**...

Pili   Pues sí, me chifla. Además me encantó esa **cala**.

Pepa   Y a mí. Con su **arena** finita y blanca y el agua **cristalina** que parecía el Caribe... Podríamos volver allí ahora.

Pili   *¡Ni hablar!* Está subiendo **la marea**. Imagínate que nos quedamos atrapadas allí, sin **socorrista** ni nada. *¡Me da un ataque!*

Pepa   Así que te quieres quedar aquí con todos los **veraneantes** de Madrid, *luciendo* sus **trajes de baño** y **gafas de sol**.

Pili   No me importaría. Se está muy bien aquí tomando *un refresco* **a la sombra**.

Pepa   Sí, es **un chiringuito** *con encanto*. Bueno, ¿**nos pegamos un baño** o pedimos algo más?

¿Lo has captado?

_____ 1. According to Pili, the guy who has just entered is:
a. a great surfer
b. a nice guy
c. really cute

_____ 2. Pepa advises Pili to:
a. get better at surfing
b. take up surfing
c. devote her life to surfing

_____ 3. Pili doesn't want to do this because she:
a. hates waves
b. isn't a sporty type
c. would rather do her surfing on the web

_____ 4. That morning on the beach:
a. the waves were really pounding
b. the sun was really strong
c. the water was really cold

_____ 5. That morning on the beach, Pili:
a. took a quick dip
b. had a cold beer
c. got really tan

_____ 6. When Pepa says that Pili is a *lagarto*, this means she's:
a. really lazy
b. a sun worshiper
c. a terrible swimmer

_____ 7. Pili doesn't want to go back to the cove because:
a. the tide's coming in
b. there's no lifeguard
c. both *a* and *b*

_____ 8. A *chiringuito* is:
a. an ice-cream stand
b. a parasol
c. an outdoor restaurant

Zooming in on the beach . . . Why are we devoting a unit to the beach? Take a wild guess . . . Yes, Spain is invaded annually by beach bums and sun worshipers. And then there's Mexico, Costa Rica, Cuba, and the Dominican Republic, to mention just a few places in Latin America where you can loll on a stretch of sand till your toes curl. As for the Spanish, summer is synonymous with at least a ten-day escapade to the coast, whether it's the sun-soaked Mediterranean shores or the cooler and more rugged Atlantic. Whatever beach you end up on, here's some vocabulary that's sure to come in handy.

¡Al grano!

a la sombra	in the shade (*versus al sol = in the sun*)
apartado/a	out of the way, off the beaten track
la arena	the sand
una cala [Spain]	a cove ([var] *una calita*)
un chapuzón	a dip
un chiringuito [Spain]	an open-air restaurant or drinks stall (*a common feature on many beaches in Spain*)
como un plato [Spain]	very calm (*only used in reference to the sea*)
crema (solar)	(suntan) lotion ([syn] *bronceador*)
cristalino/a	clear, transparent
darse un baño	to take a dip ([Spain] *pegarse un baño*)
las gafas de sol [Spain]	sunglasses ([LA] *lentes de sol*)
Hace un sol de justicia [Spain]	the sun's really strong (*literally, It's a sun of justice*)
la marea	the tide (*marea baja = low tide; marea alta = high tide*)
meterse (en el agua)	to get in (the water)
una lagarto [col]	a sun worshiper (*literally, a lizard*)
una ola	a wave
pegar fuerte	to beat down hard, to strike hot (*used in reference to the sun*)
pegarse un baño [Spain]	to take a dip ([var] *darse un baño*)
un pez	a fish (*the animal, versus un pescado, fish as food*)
playero/a	(*adj*) beach (*from una playa, a beach*)
quemarse	to get burned
refrescar	to refresh, to cool down
salir (del agua)	to get out (of the water)

un/a socorrista	a lifeguard
un/a surfista	a surfer (*el surf* = *surfing*)
tomar el sol	to sunbathe, to sit or lie in the sun
un traje de baño	a swimsuit, a bathing suit
un/a veraneante	a summer vacationer (*from* **veranear**, *to spend summer vacation;* **Veranean en la Costa Brava** — *They vacation in the Costa Brava; They spend summers on the Costa Brava*)

¡Ojo!

un aire	a look, an air (*ese aire playero* = *that beach look*)
con encanto	special, with charm (*un lugar con encanto* = *a special place, a great little spot*)
crudo/a [col, Spain]	difficult (*Lo tienes crudo* is an informal version of *Lo tienes difícil/complicado*, literally, "You have it difficult." This would translate as "The outlook isn't good" or simply a sarcastic "Good luck!")
dedicarse a (algo)	to take up (something) (but *¿A qué te dedicas?* = *What do you do for a living?*)
Esto es vida	This is the life (*versus Así es la vida* = *That's life*)
lucir	to show off, to parade, to display
¡Me da un ataque!	I'd die! I'd have a heart attack!
¡Ni hablar!	No way!
¡Olvídate! [col]	Forget it! No way!
un refresco	a soft drink
¿Y qué?	So what?

¡Te toca!

Replace the words in italics with one of the words or expressions below.

cala	apartada	chapuzón	pega fuerte
cristalina	quemado	bronceador	como un plato

1. ¡Qué calor! Hoy *hace un sol de justicia*. _____

2. Estás un poco *rojo*. Deberías ponerte un poco de Aftersun.

_____

3. El mar hoy está *muy tranquilo*. No hay ni una ola. _____

4. Me encanta esta *playita*. Es una delicia. _____

5. ¡Qué *transparente* está el agua! Se ve hasta el fondo. _____

6. ¿Me pones un poco de *crema* en la espalda? _____

7. Es una playa un poco *retirada*. Por eso hay poca gente.

   _____

8. Ya está bien de tomar el sol. Venga, vamos a darnos un *baño*.

   _____

Intercambio

Tom and Pepa have decided to go for a long weekend to Cádiz.
Fill in the blanks in the dialogue below.

Tom   ¡Qué calorazo!

Pepa   Sí, aquí en agosto (1) _____
fuerte. Venga, ¿nos (2) _____
un chapuzón?

Tom   ¿Otro? Acabamos de (3) _____
del agua.

Pepa   ¿Y qué? Los baños refrescan mucho. Además,
el agua está buenísima.

Tom   Sí, además el mar está muy tranquilo hoy. No hay ni una

(4) _____ .

Pepa   Pues venga, ¡al agua!

Tom   Espera, ¿me pones un poco de crema en la espalda antes? Creo que

me estoy (5) _____ .

Pepa   Sí, estás un poco rojo. Es que hemos (6) _____
mucho el sol hoy.

Tom   Oye, y después de este baño nos vamos al chiringuito, ¿vale?

Pepa   Buena idea. Y nos tomamos algo a la (7) _____ .

21

Estoy hecha polvo

Pepa's totally beat

Pepa   ¿Sí?

Pili   ¡Qué voz tienes! ¿Estás bien?

Pepa   Pues no, **estoy hecha polvo**. Este librito **me está machacando**.

Pili   Pero, ¿no lo has terminado ya?

Pepa   Casi. Me queda el último capítulo. Pero mira, estoy **agotada**.

Pili   Oye, Pepa, lo primero es tu salud. Esos guiris que quieren aprender el español coloquial pueden esperar...

Pepa   Díselo a mi editor. Por cierto, **soñé con** él anoche.

Pili   ¿Ah sí? ¿Qué? ¿**Un sueño** erótico?

Pepa   ¡Qué graciosa! Era **una pesadilla**. Me estaba **echando una cabezada** y *de pronto* me **despierta** *a gritos* diciendo que falta el glosario.

Pili   Vaya. Oye, *no te agobies*, Pepa. El libro ya lo terminarás *a tu ritmo*.

Pepa   Pues *tengo ganas de* acabarlo ya... En fin, anoche casi **no pegué ojo**.

Pili   ¿Qué pasa? ¿Te quedaste trabajando hasta **las tantas**?

Pepa   Sí, hija, hasta las cinco de **la madrugada**. Y hoy estoy **rota**.

Pili   Claro. Anda, métete en la cama y **échate una siesta** como Dios manda.

Pepa   No, si **me acuesto** ahora, voy a **quedarme frita** durante horas.

Pili   Pues **túmbate** un ratito en el sofá.

Pepa   Buena idea. En fin, creo que este último diálogo va a quedar un poco pesado.

Pili   *¿De qué va?*

Pepa   Pues justo de lo que estamos hablando. Del **cansancio**, del **sueño**, del **agotamiento**, de que **no doy abasto**... Bueno, venga, hasta luego...

¿Lo has captado?

_____ 1. Pepa and Pili are talking:
   a. on the phone
   b. at Pepa's place
   c. at Pili's place

_____ 2. When Pepa says she's *hecha polvo*, this means she's:
   a. an insomniac
   b. a wreck
   c. a workaholic

_____ 3. The night before, Pepa had:
   a. slept with her editor
   b. been awakened by a phone call from her editor
   c. dreamed about her editor

_____ 4. Pili tells Pepa that she should:
   a. finish the book fast
   b. give it a snappy ending
   c. go at her own pace

_____ 5. The night before Pepa:
   a. nodded off at her computer
   b. hardly slept a wink
   c. didn't go to bed

_____ 6. Pili tells Pepa to get into bed and take:
   a. a nice long nap
   b. a little snooze
   c. a heavenly rest

_____ 7. When Pepa says she'll *quedarse frita* if she gets into bed, this means she'll:
   a. toss and turn
   b. be out like a light
   c. be too wired to sleep

_____ 8. At the end Pili asks Pepa:
   a. why the last dialogue is boring
   b. what the last dialogue is about
   c. why the last dialogue is wearing her down

Zooming in on exhaustion and sleep ... No comment. Just that Pepa's a wreck and maybe you are too at this point, so we thought this would be a good subject to finish up with. Meanwhile, hats off for getting this far, and now it's time to go out and impress your *amigos* with all you know. But wait a minute ... don't you think you deserve to put your feet up first and take a little break?

¡Al grano!

acostarse	to go to bed
agobiarse	to feel overwhelmed, burdened, or oppressed ([Spain] *No te agobies* = *Don't let it get the better of you; Don't freak out*)
agotado/a	exhausted (*agotamiento* = *exhaustion*)
cansancio	tiredness
despertar	to wake up
echar una cabezada	to have a snooze, to have a catnap
echar una siesta	to have a nap after lunch
estar hecho/a polvo [col]	to be a wreck (*physically or emotionally; not to be confused with* echar un polvo, *which is a colloquial expression meaning "to get laid"*)
machacar [col]	to wear down, to put through the grinder (*literally, to crush or to grind*)
la madrugada	early morning, dawn, daybreak (*madrugar* = *to get up early*)
No doy abasto	I can't cope; It's more than I can handle
no pegar ojo	to not sleep a wink
una pesadilla	a nightmare
quedarse frito/a [col]	to be out like a light, to fall asleep, to nod off
roto/a [col, Spain]	exhausted, beat ([syn] *destrozado/a*)
soñar con (alguien)	to dream about (someone)
sueño	sleepiness (*tener sueño* = *to be tired*)
un sueño	a dream
las tantas	the wee hours, very late at night or very early in the morning
tumbarse	to lie down

¡Ojo!

a gritos	shouting
a tu ritmo	at your own pace
de pronto	suddenly

¿De qué va? [Spain]	What's it about? ([syn] *¿De qué trata?*)
tener ganas de (hacer algo)	to feel like (doing something); to really want (to do something); to be eager (to do something) (*This is an extremely common expression, which translates differently in English depending on the context.* **Tengo ganas de terminar este trabajo** = *I really want to finish up this job;* **Tengo ganas de ir al cine** = *I feel like going to the cinema;* **Tengo muchas ganas de verte** = *I can't wait to see you.*)

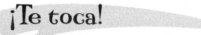

¡Te toca!

Replace the words in italics with a synonym from below.

acostar	una pesadilla	frito	No doy más abasto
rota	no pegué ojo	las tantas	una cabezada

1. Me he quedado *dormido* en el sofá viendo la tele. _____

2. Anoche *no pude dormir*. _____

3. Estoy muy cansado. Me voy a *meter en la cama* ya. _____

4. He hecho todo lo que puedo. *No puedo más.* _____

5. Estuve anoche de juerga hasta *las cuatro de la mañana.*

   _____

6. Llevo diez horas trabajando, y estoy *agotada*. _____

7. Tuve *un sueño horrible* anoche. _____

8. Después de comer me gusta echarme *una siestecita.*

   _____

Intercambio

Tom and Pili meet up later that day for their *intercambio*. Fill in the blanks as you read the dialogue.

Pili　Tom, estoy un poco preocupada por Pepa...

Tom　Sí, yo también.

Pili　Es que está (1) _____

_____. A ver si termina ese libro ya.

Tom　Pues anoche estuvo trabajando hasta las (2) _____.

Casi no (3) _____ ojo.

Pili　Ya me lo ha dicho. Y seguro que hoy tampoco se ha echado una siesta.

Tom　No, pero una pequeña (4) _____, sí. Se quedó

(5) _____ en el sofá viendo las noticias.

Pili　Vaya. Por cierto, Tom, ¿sabes que hablas ya casi como un nativo?

Tom　Gracias. En fin, he aprendido un montón contigo. Y claro, estando con Pepa también.

Pili　Sí, la verdad es que has tenido unas profes como Dios manda.

¡Ah!, por cierto, anoche soñé (6) _____ nuestro intercambio.

Tom　Algo agradable, espero.

Pili　Pues no, era más bien una (7) _____. Fíjate, soñé que tu acababas hablando un español perfecto y yo casi no sabía ni una palabra de inglés.

Tom　Vaya. Oye, no te (8) _____, Pili. Cada uno va a su ritmo, y has avanzado bastante últimamente.

Pili　¿Tú crees? Mira, Tom, no sé si valgo para los idiomas.

Tom　¡No seas boba! Come on, let's switch to English now ...

Answer Key

1 ¡Me chiflas!

¿Lo has captado?
1. b   2. b   3. c   4. a   5. b   6. b   7. c   8. c

¡Te toca!
1. me encanta   2. quiero   3. me caen bien   4. adoro   5. me gustan
6. estoy loco/a por   7. aprecio   8. amo

Intercambio
1. me encanta   2. me gustas   3. encanto   4. me caes   5. estás   6. estoy loco

2 Nos llevamos de miedo

¿Lo has captado?
1. a   2. c   3. a   4. c   5. a   6. c   7. a

¡Te toca!
1. quedamos   2. presentado   3. saliendo   4. llevamos   5. tipo   6. novio

Intercambio
1. presenté   2. quedé   3. aventura   4. serio   5. relación   6. novia

3 ¡Qué petardo!

¿Lo has captado?
1. a   2. a   3. c   4. a   5. b   6. b   7. a

¡Te toca!
1. no soporto   2. le cae muy mal   3. odio   4. no me gustan nada
5. una pesada   6. un imbécil   7. poner a parir   8. me saca de quicio

Intercambio
1. mete   2. a mis espaldas   3. me cae   4. de quicio   5. enferma *or* mala
6. no lo soporto   7. insoportable *or* inaguantable

4 ¡Es la monda!

¿Lo has captado?
1. b   2. c   3. c   4. a   5. b   6. c   7. b

¡Te toca!
1. genial   2. bestiales   3. pesado   4. espantó   5. maravilla   6. espantoso
7. original   8. fuerte

The -ísimo quiz

1. buenísimo/a   3. pesadísimo/a   4. malísimo/a   7. divertidísimo/a
8. graciosísimo/a
(*No hard and fast rules here, but just as you wouldn't say "very great" or "extremely fantastic" in English, you wouldn't add -ísimo to a word that already has "punch" such as* bestial, genial, maravilloso/a, increíble, horrorosa/a, *etc.*)

5 Eres una fresca...

¿Lo has captado?

1. b   2. c   3. a   4. b   5. c   6. b   7. a

¡Te toca!

1. tengo   2. está   3. calor   4. hace (mucho) calor   5. ¡Qué frío...!
6. caliente   7. hace   8. (un/a) caluroso/a

Intercambio

1. tienes calor   2. tengo   3. hace mucho calor   4. fresca   5. tiene frío
6. resfriado   7. caliente

6 Pareces otra

¿Lo has captado?

1. c   2. a   3. a   4. a   5. b   6. a   7. a

¡Te toca!

1. estar (*Estás muy guapo hoy.*)   2. ser (*Mi hermana es alta y morena.*)
3. ser (*¡Buenos Aires es precioso!*)   4. estar (*Está en la calle Barbieri.*)
5. estar (*¡Qué bonita está tu casa!*)
(**Ser** *is used to describe general characteristics or features of people, things, and places.* **Estar** *is used to talk about temporary states or phenomena, and to express location.*)

Intercambio

1. mona   2. belleza *or* hermosura   3. estás   4. te veo *or* [LA] te ves   5. eres
6. buen tipo   7. te queda

7 Entra de maravilla

¿Lo has captado?

1. b   2. a   3. a   4. b   5. c   6. c   7. a   8. b

¡Te toca!

1. entra   2. tinto   3. prueba   4. copa   5. brindis   6. alegre   7. cosecha
8. crianzas

Intercambio

1. copa   2. probar   3. brindis   4. entra   5. borracho   6. tinto   7. resaca

8 Una chupa de marca

¿Lo has captado?
1. b   2. b   3. b   4. a   5. c   6. a   7. c   8. a

¡Te toca!
1. precio   2. etiqueta   3. talla   4. queda   5. probar   6. quedo   7. queda
8. escaparate

Intercambio
1. de compras *or* de tiendas   2. probé   3. quedó *or* quedaba   4. rebajado
5. ir de   6. la compra

9 La penúltima...

¿Lo has captado?
1. b   2. a   3. c   4. b   5. a   6. a   7. c

¡Te toca!
1. marcha   2. ronda   3. tapa   4. aperitivo   5. tomar   6. juerga   7. ración
8. picar

Intercambio
1. picar   2. te mueres   3. pides   4. Oiga   5. pone *or* sirve   6. juerga
7. tomar   8. penúltima

10 ¡Nos vamos a forrar!

¿Lo has captado?
1. b   2. c   3. c   4. b   5. a   6. b   7. c

¡Te toca!
1. una pasta   2. está forrada   3. sin un duro   4. ir a medias   5. se forró
6. pasta   7. apretar el cinturón   8. he cobrado

Intercambio
1. estoy   2. gastos   3. de dinero   4. prestar   5. devuelvo *or* devolveré
6. medias   7. cobraste *or* te pagaron   8. sueldo

11 Estoy a tope

¿Lo has captado?
1. b   2. c   3. b   4. c   5. a   6. b   7. b

¡Te toca!
1. j   2. h   3. g   4. a   5. d   6. b   7. i   8. c   9. f   10. e

Intercambio
1. jefe   2. ascender   3. peces gordos   4. rentable   5. paro
6. contratar *or* coger   7. golpe   8. despedir *or* echar

12 ¡Qué chollo!

¿Lo has captado?
1. b   2. a   3. c   4. a   5. b   6. a   7. a

¡Te toca!
A. 1. cuesta   2. caro   3. bajar   4. dejar   5. da   6. llevo *or* quedo   7. paz
B. 1. un robo   2. regatear   3. una ganga   4. cuesta   5. llevo   6. tirada
7. doy por   8. un precio especial

Intercambio
1. antiguas   2. gangas   3. chollo   4. discutir *or* negociar   5. regatear
6. engañar   7. vuelta

13 Unas vacaciones de cine

¿Lo has captado?
1. a   2. b   3. c   4. c   5. c   6. c   7. a   8. b

¡Te toca!
1. virgen   2. temporada   3. excursiones   4. organizado   5. copiloto
6. monumentos   7. ruta

Intercambio
1. revelar   2. ruta   3. organizado   4. alquilasteis   5. conducen *or*
[LA] manejan   6. copiloto   7. explotada   8. temporada

14 ¡Estás como una foca!

¿Lo has captado?
1. c   2. a   3. c   4. b   5. b   6. b   7. a

¡Te toca!
1. régimen   2. apuntado a   3. cachas   4. quitarme   5. como una foca
6. adelgazar   7. engordar   8. se nota

Intercambio
1. ganado *or* engordado   2. nota   3. entro   4. apuntas   5. adelgazarás
6. forma   7. foca   8. tipito

15 ¡Nos vamos a poner moradas!

¿Lo has captado?
1. b   2. a   3. b   4. c   5. c   6. a   7. b   8. a

¡Te toca!
1. apetece   2. compartimos   3. dudando   4. pinta   5. sibarita   6. plancha
7. temporada   8. llena

Intercambio
1. en ello   2. pinta   3. buena mesa   4. plato   5. dudando   6. apetece
7. morados

16 El quinto pino

¿Lo has captado?
1. a   2. c   3. a   4. b   5. c   6. a   7. a

¡Te toca!
1. piso   2. balcones   3. luminoso   4. da   5. calefacción   6. edificio *or* mudó
7. centro   8. comunicado   9. céntrico

Intercambio
1. luminoso   2. da   3. interior   4. barrio   5. vecina   6. trasladó
7. comunicado   8. quinto pino

17 Un poco pachucha

¿Lo has captado?
1. a   2. b   3. c   4. c   5. b   6. b   7. a

¡Te toca!
1. encuentro   2. gripe   3. mareo   4. duele   5. mocos   6. pasa   7. baja
8. recetar

Intercambio
1. encuentro   2. dolor   3. constipada   4. sonar   5. pena   6. pastillas
7. consulta   8. me duele

18 Es una víbora...

¿Lo has captado?
1. c   2. b   3. a   4. b   5. c   6. b   7. c   8. b   9. a

¡Te toca!
1. e   2. j   3. a   4. h   5. b   6. c   7. f   8. g   9. d   10. i

Intercambio
1. simpáticos *or* majos   2. borde   3. culto   4. leche   5. manía   6. graciosa
7. hortera *or* extravagante   8. gracia

19 Los domingueros

¿Lo has captado?
1. c   2. c   3. b   4. b   5. a   6. b   7. a   8. c

¡Te toca!
1. paseo   2. pendiente   3. libre   4. domingueros   5. la sierra
6. una caminata   7. tarda   8. subir

Intercambio
1. puro   2. mochila   3. entrar *or* dar   4. subir   5. sendero *or* camino
6. a través   7. paseo   8. finca

20 Un chiringuito con encanto

¿Lo has captado?

1. c   2. b   3. a   4. b   5. a   6. b   7. c   8. c

¡Te toca!

1. pega fuerte   2. quemado   3. como un plato   4. cala   5. cristalina
6. bronceador   7. apartada   8. chapuzón

Intercambio

1. pega   2. damos   3. salir   4. ola   5. quemando   6. tomado   7. sombra

21 Estoy hecha polvo

¿Lo has captado?

1. a   2. b   3. c   4. c   5. b   6. a   7. b   8. b

¡Te toca!

1. frito   2. no pegué ojo   3. acostar   4. No doy más abasto   5. las tantas
6. rota   7. una pesadilla   8. una cabezada

Intercambio

1. hecha polvo   2. tantas   3. pegó   4. cabezada   5. frita   6. con
7. pesadilla   8. agobies

Pepa and Pili's Dialogues: English Versions

AUTHOR'S NOTE: A literal translation always sounds unnatural and forced and doesn't let you get into the spirit and feel of the other language. So these are not strict translations of Pepa and Pili's dialogues, but rather equivalents in conversational English. Reading them will help you appreciate the differences between English and Spanish, and at the same time see how and when the two languages coincide or overlap.

1 ¡Me chiflas!

Pili   Hey, Pepa, you know what? I think I'm in love again.

Pepa   No! With that guy you met the other night? That hunk?

Pili   He's a really great person. Listen, I'm crazy about him.

Pepa   Uh oh! Well, just don't go and lose your head over that Don Juan.

Pili   Well, I think he likes me too. I even think he's a little hooked on me. Last night he told me he was madly in love with me.

Pepa   That's what they all say. Hey, Pili, watch out. You know you're the kind that falls for guys at the drop of a hat. Besides, you've just broken up with Luis and it'd probably be a good idea to wait a little before getting into another relationship.

Pili   Pepa, I love you, but you're a pain in the neck. You know I think the world of Luis, but things between us just weren't meant to last. But look, I'm really into this guy. I really think he's great. In fact, I'm convinced he's the future father of my children.

Pepa   OK, pal, but I hope you haven't told him you love him or anything like that.

Pili   Listen, doll, I may be a romantic, but I'm not a total idiot! This guy really does it for me, but nobody knows better than me that you've gotta have a deft hand when it comes to seducing men. So for now, no way— I'm just gonna have a good time. After all, life is short . . .

2 Nos llevamos de miedo

Pepa   So you're still seeing that guy, huh?

Pili   Yeah, and things are going pretty well. Just think, we've already been going out for three months.

Pepa   That's right. I remember you guys got together around Easter, and it's already July. Incredible!

Pili	Yeah it is, isn't it? And we get along really great. What's more, it seems like things are getting serious.
Pepa	And here I thought you guys weren't going to last, that it was just a spring fling.
Pili	No way. I've got a real boyfriend at last. In fact, I'm still convinced he's the man of my dreams.
Pepa	Lucky you, Pili! I hope I find a guy too one of these days.
Pili	Yeah, it's about time. You broke up with Javi a year ago, and you haven't gotten involved with anyone since then. Not even a little fling to raise your spirits.
Pepa	You know that's not my style. Or pick-up bars either for that matter. I'd rather meet a guy in a wholesome, natural way. Through friends, in a course, at work . . .
Pili	Hey, what about that American guy I introduced you to the other day? What'd you think of him?
Pepa	Oh, he was really nice, but I don't think he's my type. Anyway, he asked for my phone number and we're gonna get together one of these days . . .

3 ¡Qué petardo!

Pili	Don't look, Pepa, but the creepiest guy on earth has just walked in . . .
Pepa	Oh, I know who you mean—that guy in the orange shirt. You're totally right, he's a real jerk. I can't stand him either.
Pili	Don't look at him! If he comes up to our table, I'm gonna get sick. I really can't take that guy.
Pepa	Me neither. And he's a big gossip, too. You know, the kind that trashes everyone behind their backs.
Pili	Oh, that's something else I really hate. Anyway, everyone knows he's a total jerk! And he's an arrogant bastard too.
Pepa	Yeah, he's a totally disgusting human being. And I don't like his smile either. It's as fake as the color of your hair.
Pili	Hey, hands off my new look! It cost me an arm and a leg.
Pepa	Relax, you know I didn't mean anything by that. Come on, finish your beer and let's get out of here before that asshole sees us.
Pili	He already has. He's walking over here! Oh my God, Pepa, I'm really gonna be sick! Come on, pay the waiter and let's get out of here fast . . .

4 ¡Es la monda!

Pepa   What did you think of the movie?

Pili   I thought it was terrible. A total downer. And that guy—the main character—was really repulsive. God, was he disgusting!

Pepa   Well, I thought he was a great actor and, OK, the movie was a little hard to take, but very well-made. Did you really think it was that bad?

Pili   Oh please! It was about as awful as they get. Promise you won't do this to me again.

Pepa   Hold on, it was your idea to go see it. Besides, it got rave reviews and that actor's really wonderful. OK, so the plot was a little disturbing . . .

Pili   Look, the only thing I liked was that guy's first girlfriend. What a great actress! And of course the creep kills her almost immediately.

Pepa   OK, OK, next time we'll see a comedy. Hey, we could go see Almodóvar's new movie. They say it's a lot of fun.

Pili   Oh come on, Almodóvar's a total bore! I liked two or three of his films, the rest are really tedious and irritating. Face it, the guy's passé and there's just nothing original or funny about him anymore.

Pepa   Well, I really loved his last movie. I got a real kick out of it.

Pili   Oh really? The only kick I got out of it was when the final credits came up. Look, I'll pass on Almodóvar, but I'd be into seeing the Woody Allen flick. They say it's a real blast.

Pepa   OK, you're on.

5 Eres una fresca...

Pili   Boy, it's cold in here, Pepa! I'm freezing to death!

Pepa   Come on! It's so hot outside you could bake alive! Thank God we found this place. This cool air feels really great!

Pili   You're a total Eskimo, kiddo. Come on, it feels like we're at the North Pole! You're just really warm-blooded.

Pepa   And you're a cold-blooded pain in the neck.

Pili   Yup, I've got to admit, I love it when it's nice and hot in the summer. Look, either they turn off the air conditioning or I'm gonna get a really nasty cold.

Pepa   Oh, give me a break! Have your soup or it'll get cold.

Pili   It's already cold. It's gazpacho, doll.

Pepa   Well then, get them to heat it up for you, you big pain.

Pili   That's enough, Pepa! I really am freezing! Touch my hand and you'll see.

Pepa   Hey, you're right, you're as cold as ice. Come on, forget the gazpacho and order a soup, and get them to bring it steaming hot.

Pili	Good idea, though I doubt it'll be as steamy as the waiter, who hasn't stopped staring at me. I'm gonna smile and show him a little leg, just to see how he reacts . . .
Pepa	You brazen thing. Stop it or you're gonna get the guy all worked up.
Pili	Well, let's get out of here then. I really can't handle these arctic temperatures anymore. Come on, get the check and let's go look for an outdoor café in the sun.

6 Pareces otra

Pili	Wow, you look great, Pepa! You look really different.
Pepa	What do you mean? Do I usually look that awful?
Pili	Of course not, stupid. Come on, you know you're attractive and you have a good body. But today you're looking really radiant. Besides, that jacket looks really good on you.
Pepa	I got it on sale the other day. It's nice, isn't it?
Pili	Yeah, very cute. And that color really suits you.
Pepa	You think so? It's a little flashy, but anyway . . . By the way, that bag you're carrying is really cute. Where did you get it?
Pili	In this really cool shop on Fuencarral Street. They've got some really cute and funky stuff. But hey, Pepa, how come you're all dressed up today? Are you seeing Tom later?
Pepa	Yeah, as a matter of fact. We're going to have dinner at a Moroccan restaurant that's supposed to be really good, and I think the place is a little on the fancy side.
Pili	Is it the one on Recoletos Street?
Pepa	How'd you know?
Pili	'Cuz it's the only one that fits that description. Well, Pepa . . . the place is great, you'll see. And not only is the décor gorgeous but the waiters are total hunks. I'm so jealous! You're gonna have a really great time!

7 Entra de maravilla

Pili	Hey, Pepa, I'm already wasted, and we haven't even gotten to the Rioja and Ribera del Duero vintages . . .
Pepa	But didn't you hear the teacher? You're supposed to just try a little and then spit it out . . .
Pili	I can't, Pepa. This spitting out business is really gross. Besides, everything's so damn good . . .
Pepa	Anyway, you're supposed to sip wine, not gulp it back. Come on, have a glass of water. It'll go down really well right now.
Pili	What really went down great was that red Chilean wine. God, was it good! Do you remember the name of the vineyard?

Pepa   No, I don't, but I remember the year. It was a '94 special vintage. And it really was great. In fact, I'm gonna head over to the liquor store tomorrow and buy a couple of bottles.

Pili   Yeah, that way you and Tom will have something to toast with. Isn't it his birthday tomorrow?

Pepa   You're right, I'd forgotten. Well, we're going to make a toast with a *real* wine.

Pili   Go for it! Hey, Pepa, aren't you just a little tipsy from all the wine we've been trying?

Pepa   No, actually. But of course I haven't been drinking everything that's been poured into my glass, or I'd be really drunk.

Pili   You're a real bore, Pepa! A total party pooper! Come on, pass me that pitcher of water. . . . I get the feeling I'm gonna have a really nasty hangover tomorrow. . . .

8 Una chupa de marca

Pili   How do these jeans look on me?

Pepa   A little on the tight side. You should probably go for the next size up.

Pili   Are you kidding? Tight-fitting is in. Look, I'm gonna get them, seeing as they're really marked down.

Pepa   You're nuts! You've already got tons of clothes.

Pili   Listen, Pepa, I only go shopping during the sales, so just leave me alone.

Pepa   OK, OK. But come on, don't try on anything else.

Pili   Hold on, there's just this jacket. Hey! The price tag's missing . . .

Pepa   No big deal. The clerk'll know what it costs.

Pili   Well, you go ask her the price, OK? She gave me a really dirty look when I came into the changing room.

Pepa   No wonder. You had ten items of clothing when the maximum is six.

Pili   Hey, while you're at it, ask her if they've got that handbag that's in the window in black.

(Several minutes later)

Pepa   That jacket costs sixty euros. A bit of a rip-off, huh?

Pili   Yeah, but it's a designer label. That's pretty reasonable. And what did she say about the bag?

Pepa   There are none left in black. Come on, hurry up, they're gonna close the store any minute.

(Afterwards, on the street)

Pepa   Listen, that's the last time I go shopping with you. And to top it all off, everything's closed now and I can't do the grocery shopping.

Pili   Relax, I'll treat you to lunch, OK? Hey, can you give me a hand with these bags? They weigh a ton.

9 La penúltima

Pepa   These olives are great!

Pili   I told you they had really delicious *tapas* here. Come on, try the *patatas bravas* too, they're awesome.

Pepa   You're right, and this little *caña* is really good . . .

Pili   Yeah, they really know how to pull beer here.

Pepa   Well, well, we'll just have to come here more often for the *aperitivo*.

Pili   Hey, should we get something else to snack on? How about an order of anchovies in vinegar?

Pepa   Sounds good to me . . .

Pili   (*To the waiter*) Excuse me! Can we have an order of anchovies in vinegar, please!

(*Several minutes later*)

Pepa   Well, Pili, that was some wild night!

Pili   Yeah, it was great. And that Irish guy at the bar in Huertas was really hilarious.

Pepa   That guy that was imitating Travolta? Boy, was he revved up. I got exhausted just watching him dance.

Pili   Me too. And here I thought these gringo types were real bores.

Pepa   Well, that one definitely wasn't. So? Did you like him?

Pili   A little. Anyway, we're gonna get together this week to go out for a drink and a bite to eat.

Pepa   Oh yeah? What about your boyfriend, Pili?

Pili   Paco? He's always out and about partying with his friends! Go figure!

Pepa   You're right, he pushes it a little. Anyway, how about another beer?

Pili   OK, one for the road. (*To the waiter*) Excuse me! Can we have one more round, please!

10 ¡Nos vamos a forrar!

Pili   Pepa, can you lend me fifty euros? I'm really broke.

Pepa   But didn't you just get paid a few days ago?

Pili   Yeah, but I spent a fortune on the sales. And I won't even go into my phone bill. It almost gave me a heart attack . . .

Pepa   That doesn't surprise me. That's what you get for having a boyfriend that lives in Ireland.

Pili   That's my business, pal. Come on, I'll pay you back next week.

Pepa	Here you go, fifty euros . . . but you're an idiot. You should've stayed with the guy you were seeing before. He was really loaded.
Pili	Well, he acted like he was rich, but he never had any money on him. In fact, we almost always went Dutch.
Pepa	So . . . a cheapskate . . . yuck! Then again, it's pretty normal these days to pay one's own way.
Pili	Yeah, but guys earn more and besides, they don't have any expenses. Since they all live with Mommy and Daddy . . .
Pepa	Yeah, they've got a lot of nerve.
Pili	So tell me, Pepa, how come you're never strapped for cash?
Pepa	'Cuz I deposit part of my salary into a savings account that I only touch when I'm in a bind.
Pili	That's very sensible of you! Anyway, Pepa, I'm fed up with always being broke.
Pepa	So tighten your belt and save a little, sister.
Pili	I can't. I've got a better idea. Let's play the lottery.
Pepa	Don't be stupid! That's throwing money out the window.
Pili	Hey, you never know. . . . Come on, Pepa, we're gonna hit the jackpot!

11 Estoy a tope

Pili	I've had it, Pepa. I need a vacation.
Pepa	Me too. Working this hard isn't good for your health.
Pili	You said it! I haven't let up for a while now. And today I spent the entire morning glued to my computer without taking a break.
Pepa	What about your coworkers? Are they swamped too?
Pili	Are you kidding? I'm up to my ears and there they are chatting away. They don't lift a finger.
Pepa	Oh well. What about that new girl you just hired?
Pili	Her? She got in because some strings were pulled. They hired her 'cuz her dad's friends with the president. And she spends the whole day brownnosing the boss. It's enough to make you puke. . . .
Pepa	I hear you.
Pili	Anyway, I've had it with my job. And I can't take my boss anymore.
Pepa	What are you saying? You've always gotten along well with Arturo.
Pili	Yeah, but ever since he got promoted and became a head honcho in the company, he's been unbearable.
Pepa	Oh dear.
Pili	Anyway, I'm really burned out. With a little luck I'll get myself fired.
Pepa	And what would you do if they laid you off? Live off unemployment benefits?

Pili Yeah, while I get my act together. And then I'd probably start up my own company. Something profitable, of course.

Pepa You're nuts! How would you do it? You don't have any capital. . . .

Pili Listen, that's the least of it. . . . You just wait, Pepa, I'm going to make it!

12 ¡Qué chollo!

Pepa Keep an eye on your bag, there are these two shady types just behind us.

Pili Oh yeah? Well, I've already been robbed once in the Rastro, and if they try it again, they're gonna get it. . . .

Pepa We're safe. They've split.

Pili Hey, Pepa, what a cool table! Do you see it?

Pepa Yeah, it's nice. Come on, ask them what they want for it.

Pili OK, I'll be right back. . . . (*Two minutes later*) 150 euros. Pretty steep, huh?

Pepa Yeah, a real rip-off. Come on, offer him half and see what he says.

Pili No way, Pepa! I'm lousy at bargaining.

Pepa So drop it then. How about we take a stroll and look at some more stalls?

Pili Hold on! Do you really think he'd come down on the price?

Pepa You've got nothing to lose by trying.

Pili Fine, but come with me and help me bring him down, OK?

(*They go up to the vendor*)

Pepa Listen, if you give it to us for seventy-five euros, we'll take it.

Vendor Let me tell you something, miss. This table's an antique. It belonged to my great-grandparents.

Pepa Oh come on! Don't try to con me. It's made of pine and it's ten years old at most.

Vendor Look, I'm going to give your friend a special deal. Gimme one hundred euros and we'll call it even.

Pepa No way. Eighty euros, last offer. Come on, Pili, there are some more tables over there . . .

Vendor All right, all right, give me eighty-five.

(*Several minutes later*)

Pili That was a real steal! What a bargain!

Pepa Yeah, it was a real deal in the end. And this little table's gonna look really cute in your living room.

13 Unas vacaciones de cine

Pili   So did you see a lot of Mayan ruins?

Pepa   Of course . . . We combed the whole Yucatan.

Pili   Hey, this building's really gorgeous!

Pepa   Oh yeah, that's Mérida. We went there first to walk around the city and do some sightseeing. And from there we did the whole Mayan route.

Pili   Wow, that sounds great! And how did you get from one place to another?

Pepa   Well, it was tricky. Since we didn't go on a package tour, we took the local buses at the beginning. And that was a real pain, so then we rented a car.

Pili   Oh yeah? I hope Tom didn't drive . . .

Pepa   Well, he drove a little at the beginning and almost got us killed. The rest of the trip he was in the passenger seat.

Pili   Thank God for that. Because if you were knocking back tequilas as well . . .

Pepa   No way! We hardly drank at all. And we went to bed early every day to take advantage of the daylight hours and do day trips.

Pili   Hey, what a beach, Pepa! Wow!

Pepa   Oh yeah, that's in Tulum.

Pili   Where are the tourists? It looks totally deserted.

Pepa   Well, that area's really unspoiled, and the coast hasn't been developed at all. Besides, it was the off-season. That's also why we got the flight so cheap.

Pili   Wow, you've really had some vacation. My God, Pepa, how many rolls did you take?

Pepa   Five, I think. There are three more that haven't been developed yet.

Pili   You're too much! Oh, and this snapshot of Tom eating guacamole is really a riot! He looks like a total gringo . . .

14 ¡Estás como una foca!

Pepa   Hey, you didn't use to have that tummy, Pili.

Pili   Or these love handles either. And the worst of it is I can't get into my clothes anymore.

Pepa   Yup, you look like a fat pig, kiddo.

Pili   Oh come on, Pepa! I've put on five kilos max.

Pepa   Yeah, but since you have a small frame, it shows more. Look, it's no big deal. Just go on a diet and you'll lose the weight in a month.

Pili   Yeah, in fact tomorrow I'm starting a macrobiotic diet.

Pepa	That's a little radical. Look, just cut out the beer and bread and eat healthy. You know, lots of veggies and fish and easy on the fat.
Pili	Well, we'll see. Anyway, guess what? I've joined a gym.
Pepa	Oh yeah? Well, you'll see, there's nothing like doing a little exercise to feel good and get into shape.
Pili	I totally agree. Today I went to the aerobics class and spent an hour jumping up and down and sweating like a pig. And then I got into the steam room. It's great. You really come out feeling brand new.
Pepa	Of course, 'cuz you get rid of all those toxins . . .
Pili	And get this, Pepa, the gym's full of all these total hunks. They're all over the place, walking on the treadmill, lifting weights . . .
Pepa	I thought you weren't into guys with a lot of muscles.
Pili	Well, not the Schwarzenegger type, but a little healthy and robust is very virile. And the monitor's a real Adonis.
Pepa	Yeah, and I bet he's gay. Look, get serious and start peeling off those kilos. And you'll see, you'll get your figure back in no time.

15 ¡Nos vamos a poner moradas!

Pili	That's it, Pepa. I'm breaking my diet today.
Pepa	Great, so let's pig out! Have you looked at the menu?
Pili	Hold on, I'm working on it. Hey, the lunch special looks really good.
Pepa	Yeah, Juan recommended it and you know how obsessive he is about good food.
Pili	Yeah, obsessive and obese. The guy's really huge.
Pepa	Yeah, he overdoes it like most of these gourmet types. Plus he's got a real sweet tooth.
Pili	That's why he likes this place. They've got some really delicious cakes.
Pepa	Really? Uh oh! Anyway, what are you going to have to start?
Pili	I don't know. I'm trying to make up my mind between the gazpacho and the stuffed red peppers.
Pepa	Come on, order the peppers. That way we can share.
Pili	I don't trust you. Since you're a total glutton, you're gonna end up eating everything.
Pepa	You know, you can be really unpleasant sometimes. We'll split the dish down the middle, OK?
Pili	All right. What are you going to get as a starter?
Pepa	The grilled asparagus. It's in season now.
Pili	Hey, Pepa, what's that they're eating at the table next to us? It smells incredible.
Pepa	It's a Madrid-style stew, I think.

Pili	Oh no, that's really filling. And since the whole mad cow business started, I'm totally off meat . . .
Pepa	But that was years ago, stupid. Besides, that stew's almost all pork.
Pili	I don't care. Besides, it's really rich and I feel like having something light as a main course. That way I'll have room for dessert.
Pepa	Good thinking. Oh look! Here comes the waiter . . .

16 El quinto pino

Pepa	Hey, Pili, how was that apartment you saw today?
Pili	A real dump. Dark, small, facing onto an airshaft. And expensive to boot.
Pepa	Oh dear. Anyway, they say rents have gone up a lot recently. It's probably not a good time to be apartment-hunting.
Pili	Listen, Pepa, I've got no choice. My landlord sold the place where I'm living and I have a month to find something.
Pepa	Well, you better jump on it, pal. Haven't you seen anything you like?
Pili	Yeah, an attic apartment around the Latina, but of course it was beyond my budget.
Pepa	Don't worry, you'll find some deal. Is that today's *Segunda Mano*?
Pili	Yeah. Wanna take a look at it?
Pepa	Come on. Let's see, apartments for rent, four hundred to six hundred euros. Hey, look at this, small attic apartment, centrally located, furnished, kitchenette, very cute.
Pili	Pepa, do you know what a top floor apartment's like in the summer? You die of heat! And in the winter you freeze. Listen, no way . . .
Pepa	OK, OK. What about this one? Studio in renovated building, central heating, elevator, balcony onto the street, lots of light.
Pili	That sounds pretty good. Is it downtown?
Pepa	No, it's in Aluche. But that area's not bad. And it's got really good public transportation.
Pili	Come on, that's way the hell out! I wouldn't live there even if I were crazy!
Pepa	OK, fine. Hold on, come to think of it, my neighbor's moving to Vigo next month. And I think her apartment's up for grabs.
Pili	Oh yeah? I love your neighborhood. Come on, let's call her right away. . . .

17 Un poco pachucha

Pili   Hello?

Pepa   It's me, Pepa. Have you gotten over your cold?

Pili   Are you kidding? I want to die. I really feel terrible.

Pepa   I'm a little under the weather too. It must be a virus that's going around.

Pili   Hold on, don't hang up. I have to blow my nose . . .

(Several seconds later)

Pepa   You're a real wreck, kiddo.

Pili   Tell me about it! And apart from a runny nose, my throat hurts like hell. Can you believe it? I can barely even swallow liquid.

Pepa   Don't worry, it's just a bad cold. Besides, it's that time of year. Everyone's sick these days.

Pili   Listen, sweets, this is more than a cold. Last night I felt so faint I almost passed out. I swear to God I was about to go to the emergency room.

Pepa   Yeah, but you get dizzy a lot. Since you have low blood pressure . . .

Pili   You're no comfort at all, you know. You're just like my doctor at the clinic yesterday who told me this wasn't anything serious. Get this, the pig refused to give me sick leave.

Pepa   Of course! He must have realized that you're a total hypochondriac. Anyway, didn't he prescribe anything for you?

Pili   Yeah, some pills and cough syrup. And up to now they haven't done anything. Listen, Pepa, what I have is a really nasty flu and that's that. Besides, just talking to you is giving me a headache.

Pepa   Hey, don't get nasty. Do you want me to come over and bring you some magazines?

Pili   Yeah! Come on, get the latest *Hola*. That'll definitely be therapeutic.

18 Es una víbora...

Pepa   What a tacky guy! Get a load of that fur coat he's wearing.

Pili   OK, it's a little flamboyant, but I think it's fun. Besides, apparently he's a real liberal.

Pepa   I've also heard he's a selfish pig and has a really nasty temper. . . .

Pili   Of course, like every artist. Look, you're not gonna change my mind. I really like that guy. Besides, he's really hot.

Pepa   You think he's attractive? Oh well, there's no accounting for taste.

Pili   It's his wife that gives me the creeps. She's a real viper. . . .

Pepa   Actually she's really bright and on the ball. Apparently she's really good at what she does.

Pili   Give me a break! She's just out for herself and besides, she acts like a prima donna.

Pepa	Listen, you just don't like her because she's with him. Anyway, let's stop looking at *Hola* and talk about your party. OK, who are you going to invite?
Pili	I don't know, it's gonna be difficult. My new place fits thirty people max.
Pepa	Well, let's make up a list then. Paco, Teresa, Mónica, Manolo, Pedro, Ana . . .
Pili	Ana, no, she's a real party pooper. I only want to have fun people.
Pepa	OK, so she's a little serious but she's a nice person. At least she seems nice to me.
Pili	Oh yeah? Well, when she drinks she can get really rude. It's pretty unpleasant.
Pepa	OK, so forget Ana. What about José Luis? You can't say he's not funny and outgoing.
Pili	Yeah, he's a really great guy. And really smart too. But his girlfriend's a real weirdo. . . .
Pepa	You're right. At first she seems all sweet and polite, but then she's a real jealous bitch. And she can be pretty nasty, too.
Pili	Yup, she's a bit of a witch. Anyway, he's not exactly a saint either. Come on, add them to the list, they'll liven things up. Every party needs to have a little excitement. . . .

19 Los domingueros

Pepa	Wanna climb that hill?
Pili	You're out of your mind! It's covered in brush and there's no path.
Pepa	So what? We'll go cross-country. It's more fun . . .
Pili	No way, Pepa! It's really steep. It'd take us a couple of hours to get to the top.
Pepa	But didn't you want to do some serious hiking?
Pili	Yeah, but not with that much uphill. Besides, it's one o'clock already and I'm getting really hungry.
Pepa	Oh, come on! You're just like those Sunday day-trippers who come to the mountains, take a half-hour stroll, then say, "Hey, it's time for lunch."
Pili	Well, to be honest, I wouldn't mind stopping somewhere to have a bite to eat. . . .
Pepa	But aren't you carrying food in your backpack?
Pili	Yeah, but not a nice cold beer.
Pepa	Oh come on! Stop being a pain and enjoy the countryside a little.
Pili	You have a point. It feels really great to breathe this fresh mountain air.
Pepa	You said it. Especially after all the pollution in Madrid.
Pili	You know what? I'd really love to run a rural bed and breakfast. Somewhere off the beaten track where you can do outdoor sports.

Pepa	But you're a total city rat! You'd go crazy after two days.
Pili	I see you don't know my rural side. Hey, Pepa, this is private property, right?
Pepa	Yeah, I just saw a sign that said private hunting grounds.
Pili	That must be the ranch next door. There are wild bulls here, pal!
Pepa	You're kidding!
Pili	No, I'm serious. See that one behind the tree over there? Come on, let's get out of here fast. . . .

20 Un chiringuito con encanto

Pepa	This is the life. Sitting here and looking out at the horizon.
Pili	I'm not looking that far. That surfer who just came in is really hot.
Pepa	A little young for you, wouldn't you say? He can't be a day over twenty.
Pili	So what? He's tall and handsome. And that beach look just kills me.
Pepa	So take up surfing, kiddo. You've got a reason now.
Pili	No way, I hate waves. I like the sea when it's calm as a sheet.
Pepa	Then I think you'll have to kiss your surfer goodbye. By the way, you got a little burned.
Pili	Yeah, I forgot to put on sun block this morning.
Pepa	You're nuts! The sun was really beating down hard in that little cove.
Pili	Yeah, it was really strong. But that dip really cooled me down.
Pepa	Oh come on! You got in for a second and got out immediately . . .
Pili	That was quite enough. I don't need to stay in the water for half an hour like you. I bet you were a fish in a former life.
Pepa	And I bet you were a lizard. The way you lounge in the sun . . .
Pili	Yup, I just love it. And I really loved that beach too.
Pepa	Me too. With its wonderful, fine white sand and that clear water that looked like the Caribbean. . . . Wanna go back there now?
Pili	No way, the tide's coming in. Imagine if we got trapped there, with no lifeguard or anything. I'd have a heart attack!
Pepa	So you want to stay here with all the vacationers from Madrid showing off their swimsuits and sunglasses?
Pili	I wouldn't mind. It's great to be here in the shade downing a soft drink.
Pepa	Yeah, this is a cool little beach hut. Hey, wanna go for a dip or shall we get something else?

21 Estoy hecha polvo

Pepa   Hello?

Pili   What's wrong with your voice? Are you OK?

Pepa   No, I'm a wreck. This little book's really wearing me out.

Pili   I thought you'd already finished it.

Pepa   Almost. One more chapter to go. But I'm really exhausted.

Pili   Listen, Pepa, your health comes first. Those gringos that want to learn conversational Spanish can wait.

Pepa   You tell my editor that. By the way, I dreamt about him last night.

Pili   Oh yeah? What? Some erotic fantasy?

Pepa   Very funny. It was a nightmare. I was taking a catnap when all of a sudden he wakes me up screaming that the glossary's missing.

Pili   Oh dear . . . Look, just chill out, Pepa. You'll finish the book in your own time.

Pepa   But I just want to get it over with. Anyway, last night I hardly slept a wink.

Pili   How come? Were you up working till some Godforsaken hour?

Pepa   Yup, till five in the morning. And today I'm really beat.

Pili   No wonder! Come on, get yourself into bed and take a nice long nap.

Pepa   No, if I get into bed now I'll be out like a light for hours.

Pili   So lie down on the sofa for a while.

Pepa   Good idea. Anyway, I think this last dialogue's going to be pretty boring.

Pili   What's it about?

Pepa   Well, just what we're talking about. Tiredness, sleepiness, exhaustion, and my not being able to put out any more effort. Listen, I'll talk to you later, OK?

Spanish-English Glossary

This glossary contains all the vocabulary that appears in bold and/or italics in Pepa and Pili's dialogues. Note that the translations provided here are contextual and that some of the words listed have other meanings as well.

Key to abbreviations

adj	adjective
adv	adverb
dim	diminutive
n	noun (with both feminine and masculine forms)
nf	feminine noun
nm	masculine noun
pl	plural
v	verb

[col]	colloquial word or expression used in most Latin American countries and Spain
[col, Spain]	colloquial word or expression used in Spain
[LA]	word or expression used in most of Latin America
[Spain]	only in Spain
[syn]	synonym used in both Latin America and Spain
[var]	variation on a word

When no abbreviation appears, the entry is simply an everyday phrase that's been translated. The bracketed numbers that follow the definition refer to the units where the word is used.

A

aceituna (*nf*) olive [9]

acostarse (*v*) to go to bed [13, 21]

adelgazar (*v*) to get thinner, to lose weight [14]

adorar (*v*) to adore [1]

agobiado/a (*adj*) overwhelmed, overloaded (*Used more in Spain than in Latin America*) [11]

agobiarse (*v*) to feel overwhelmed, burdened, or oppressed ([Spain] *No te agobies* = *Don't let it get the better of you; Don't freak out*) [21]

agotado/a (*adj*) exhausted (*agotamiento* = *exhaustion*) [21]

a gritos shouting, screaming [21]

aguantar (*v*) to put up with or bear (*No lo aguanto* = *I can't stand him*) [3, 11]

aguafiestas (*n*) party pooper [7, 18]

Ahora vuelvo I'll be right back [12]

ahorrar (*v*) to save (money, time, *etc.*) [10]

¿Ah sí? Really? Oh yeah? [3, 6, 12, 13, 14, 15, 16, 21]

aire (*nm*) look [20]

aire puro fresh air [19]

al aire libre outdoors [19]

al sol in the sun [5]

a la plancha grilled [15]

a la sombra in the shade [20]

alegre (*adj*) tipsy, drunk [7]

alquilar (*v*) to rent ([LA] *rentar* is used in some countries, such as Mexico) [13]

alquiler (*nm*) rent, rental ([LA] *renta* is used in some countries: Chile, Mexico, etc.) [16]

amar (*v*) to love [1]

amueblado/a (*adj*) furnished [16]

Anda [Spain] Come on [3, 5, 7, 9, 10, 12, 15, 17, 21]

¡Anda! [Spain] Hey! Whoa! (*as an exclamation this expresses surprise, i.e., you've just seen, realized, or discovered something*) [8]

¡Anda ya! [Spain] Come on! Don't give me that! [12, 19]

animar (**la fiesta**) (*v*) to liven up (the party) [18]

antiguo/a (*adj*) antique, old (*versus viejo/a which often has negative connotations*) [12]

apartado/a (*adj*) out of the way, off the beaten track [20]

apartamento (*nm*) [LA] apartment; [Spain] one-bedroom apartment [16]

aperitivo (*nm*) aperitif; [Spain] pre-lunch drink and snack (*See "A Spanish Institution" in Unit 9.*) [9]

apreciar (*v*) to appreciate or value (*Te aprecio conveys the idea of appreciation, respect, and fondness*) [1]

apretarse el cinturón to tighten one's belt, to economize [10]

aprovechar (*v*) to take advantage of [13]

apuntar (*v*) to write down [18]

apuntarse a (**un gimnasio**) (*v*) [Spain] to enroll or sign up at (a gym) ([syn] *matricularse or inscribirse*) [14]

apuro (*nm*) financial need, hardship (*en momentos de apuro* = when I'm hard up) [10]

¿A quién se le ocurre...? Who'd ever think of . . . ? [10]

ardiendo very hot, boiling (literally, *on fire*) [5]

arena (*nf*) sand [20]

argumento (*nm*) plot [4]

(ir/estar) arreglado/a (*adj*) (to be) smart, attractive, well-dressed [6]

artimaña (*nf*) cunning, wiles [1]

a salvo safe [12]

ascender (*v*) to promote, to give a promotion [11]

ascensor (*nm*) elevator [16]

asco (*nm*) disgust (*Me da asco* = It's disgusting; *¡Qué asco!* = How disgusting!) [4, 7]

a sus espaldas behind his/her/their back(s) [3]

a tope [col, Spain] totally, to the max (*See also estar a tope*) [4]

a tu ritmo at your own pace [21]

aventura (*nf*) an affair or fling [2]

B

baja (*nf*) [Spain] sick leave (*estar de baja* = to be on sick leave) [17]

bajar (*v*) **de peso** to lose weight [14]

bajar (*v*) **el precio** to bring down the price [12]

bajón (*nm*) a sharp drop in blood pressure, a general turn for the worse (*either physically or emotionally*) [17]

baño (*nm*) **turco** steam room [14]

barrio (*nm*) neighborhood [16]

Basta con (**hacer un poco de ejercicio**) It's enough if you (do a little exercise) [14]

una belleza (*nf*) a knock-out, really beautiful [6]

bestial (*adj*) [col] great, fantastic [4]

bien comunicado/a [Spain] with good public transport [16]

bisabuelos (*nm, pl*) great-grandparents [12]

bobo/a (*adj*) silly, stupid [10]

bodega (*nf*) wine cellar, winery, liquor store [7]

bolsa (*nf*) bag, generally large (*canvas bag, beach bag, shopping bag, etc.*) [8]

bolso (*nm*) [Spain] handbag, purse ([LA] *cartera; in Mexico, bolsa*) [6, 8, 12]

bonito/a (*adj*) nice, beautiful, lovely [6, 12, 13]

boquerones (*nm, pl*) **en vinagre** anchovies marinated in vinegar (*a typical tapa in Madrid*) [9]

borde (*adj*) [col, Spain] rude, nasty, out of line [17, 18]

borracho/a (*adj*) drunk [7]

brindar (v) to make a toast (with wine)
[7]

brindis (nm) a toast (with wine) [7]

bruja (nf) witch [18]

brutal (adj) [col, Spain] tremendous,
colossal [5, 7]

bueno/a (adj) sexy, "hot" (when used
with estar in reference to people)
[18, 20]

la buena mesa fine dining, good food
[15]

buhardilla (nf) [Spain] small attic
apartment [16]

C

cabezada (nf) snooze, catnap [21]

cachas (adj) [col, Spain] hunky, built [14]

caer (bien, mal) (v) See me cae bien
and me cae mal [1, 18]

cala (nf) [Spain] cove [20]

caldo (nm) clear hot soup (broth or
consommé) [5]

calefacción (nf) central central heating
[16]

calentar (v) to heat up, to turn on
sexually [5]

Calla [col, Spain] You're right; You said it
(among slang, literally, be quiet) [17]

calorcito (nm, dim) pleasant
warmth/heat (Hace calorcito =
It's nice and warm/hot) [5]

caluroso/a (adj and n) warm-blooded
[5]

cambiar de idea to change one's mind
[18]

caminata (nf) [Spain] a long walk, a hike
[19]

campestre (adj) country, rural [19]

campo a través cross-country [19]

caña (nf) [Spain] small glass of draft
beer ([var] cañita) [9]

cansancio (nm) tiredness [21]

carrete (nm) [Spain] a roll of film
([LA] un rollo) [13]

carta (nf) menu [15]

cartel (nm) sign [19]

casa (nf) rural [Spain] rural bed and
breakfast [19]

casero/a (n) landlord/landlady [16]

catarro (nm) cold ([var] catarrazo) [17]

céntrico/a (adj) centrally located [16]

el centro (nm) downtown, the city
center [16]

ceñido/a (adj) close-fitting, clinging [8]

cerdo (n) pork, pig (food or animal);
pig, bastard (person) [15, 17]

cerro (nm) hill [19]

chapuzón (nm) dip [20]

chiflar [col, Spain] to captivate
(Me chiflas = I think you're great) [1]

chiringuito (nm) [Spain] open-air
restaurant or drinks stall [20]

chollo (nm) [col, Spain] deal, bargain
[12, 16]

chorizo (nm) [col, Spain] small-time
crook, pickpocket [12]

chulo/a (adj) [col, Spain] cute, cool, fun
([var] una chulada) [6, 12]

chupa (nf) [col, Spain] sports jacket [8]

la cinta (nf) [Spain] the treadmill [14]

cobrar (v) to get paid [10]

cocina (nf) americana kitchenette [16]

coger (v) [Spain] to get, to hire (taboo
word in Latin America) [11]

como Dios manda proper(ly), the way
it's meant to be (una siesta como Dios
manda = a "real" siesta) [7, 21]

como mucho at most [14, 18, 20]

como una bestia [col] like crazy, a lot
[14]

como un plato [Spain] totally calm
(used in reference to the sea) [20]

compañero/a (n) de trabajo coworker,
workmate [11]

compartir (v) to share [15]

conducir (v) [Spain] to drive ([LA]
manejar) [13]

con encanto special, with charm
(un hotel con encanto = a great little
hotel) [20]

congelarse (v) to freeze [5]

conocer (v) a alguien to meet someone
(for the first time) [2]

constipado (adj and n) cold (estar
constipado/a = to have a cold, versus
estar estreñido = to be constipated)
[17]

consulta (nf) clinic, doctor's office [17]

consultorio (nm) clinic, doctor's office
[17]

contaminación (nf) pollution [19]

contratar (v) to hire [11]

copa (*nf*) glass (*for wine and alcoholic beverages*) [7]

el/la copiloto (*n*) the person in the passenger seat, the navigator [13]

coqueto/a (*adj*) [Spain] charming, cute [16]

corriendo right away, immediately [3, 16, 20]

cosecha (*nf*) year, vintage (*for wine*) [7]

costar (*v*) to cost; to require an effort (*Me cuesta hablar* = *It's hard for me to talk*) [8, 17]

un/a cotilla (*n*) [Spain] a gossip ([syn] *chismoso/a*) [3]

coto (*nm*) **de caza** [Spain] private hunting grounds [19]

crema (solar) (*nf*) [Spain] (suntan) lotion ([syn] *bronceador*) [20]

crianza (*nm*) [Spain] vintage wine [7]

cristalino/a (*adj*) clear, transparent [20]

crítica (*nf*) review [4]

crudo/a (*adj*) [col, Spain] difficult (*Lo tienes crudo*, literally, *You have it difficult, i.e., The outlook doesn't look very good*) [20]

Cuando pueda [Spain] When you have a moment (*often used when ordering food or drink*) [9]

cuchitril (*nm*) dump, rat hole [16]

cuenta (*nf*) **de ahorros** savings account [10]

cuesta arriba/abajo [Spain] uphill/downhill [19]

culto/a (*adj*) educated, knowledgeable, well-read [18]

currar (*v*) [col, Spain] to work (*el curro* = *work*) [11]

cursillo (*nm*) [Spain] a short course [2]

D

Da gusto (respirar) It feels great (to breathe) [19]

dar (*v*) to get (*for symptoms; Me da alergia en primavera*) [17]

dar a (la calle) (*v*) to face or open onto (the street) [16]

dar asco to be disgusting (*Me da asco* = *It's disgusting!*) [7]

dar un paseo to go for a walk, to take a stroll [19]

dar repelús to give the creeps [18]

darse un baño to take a dip [20]

dar una vuelta to take a stroll, to go for a walk [12]

¡Date prisa! Hurry up! [8]

de cine [col, Spain] fantastic ([syn] *de película*) [13]

dedicarse (a algo) (*v*) to take up (something) (*but ¿A qué te dedicas?* = *What do you do for a living?*) [20]

De eso nada No way! Are you kidding! [2]

de entrada (*adv*) at first, at the beginning [18]

¡Déjame en paz! Leave me alone! Let me be! [8]

¡Déjate de tonterías! Come on! Don't be ridiculous! Stop fooling around! [14]

dejar de (salir, hacer, etc.) to stop (going out with, doing, etc.) [2]

de miedo (*adj and adv*) [col, Spain] great, fantastic, really well ([syn] *de muerte*) [2, 9, 20]

de moda in fashion, "in" [8]

de mucho cuidado terrible, big (*un cotilla de mucho cuidado* = *a big gossip*) [3]

de muerte (*adj and adv*) [col] great, fantastic [15]

dependiente/a (*n*) sales clerk, shop assistant [8]

deprimente (*adj*) depressing [4]

de primer plato *or* **de primero** as a starter/appetizer/first course [15]

de pronto all of a sudden, suddenly [21]

¿De qué va? [Spain] What's it about? ([syn] *¿De qué trata?*) [21]

desagradable (*adj*) unpleasant, nasty [4, 15, 18]

de segundo plato *or* **de segundo** as an entree/main course [15]

desmayarse (*v*) to faint [17]

despedir (*v*) to lay off or dismiss [11]

despertar (*v*) to wake up [21]

desplazarse (*v*) to get from one place to another [13]

de temporada [Spain] in season [15]

devolver (v) to pay back (*for money or loaned objects*) [10]

Di que sí [col, Spain] Go for it! All right! (*used as affirmation*) [7]

discutir (v) el precio to haggle or argue over the price [12]

disfrutar (v) to enjoy oneself (*disfrutar de/con algo = to enjoy something*) [1, 19]

diva (*nf*) prima donna [18]

divertido/a (*adj*) fun, entertaining [4, 18, 19]

dolor (*nm*) de cabeza/estómago/espalda headache/stomachache/backache [17]

dominguero/a (*n*) [Spain] Sunday excursionist [19]

dulce (*adj*) gentle, sweet, kind [18]

durar (v) to last [1, 2]

E

echar (v) to lay off or fire; [Spain] to pour (*for drinks;* [LA] *servir*) [7, 11]

echar (v) una cabezada to have a snooze, to have a catnap [21]

echar una mano to give a hand, to help out [8]

echar una siesta to have a post-lunch nap [21]

echar un vistazo to take a look (*at something*) [16]

echarse un/a novio/a [col, Spain] to get oneself a boy/girlfriend [2]

edificio (*nm*) building [13, 16]

educado/a (*adj*) polite, well-mannered [18]

egoísta (*adj and n*) selfish, egotistical [18]

emocionante (*adj*) exciting [4]

emoción (*nf*) excitement [18]

emocionar (v) to excite, thrill, move, or touch (*¡Me emocionó! = I loved it! or It really hit a spot!*) [4]

empresa (*nf*) company [11]

en alquiler for rent (*en renta in some Latin American countries*) [16]

enamoradizo/a (*adj*) the type that falls in love often or easily [1]

enamorarse (v) to fall in love [1]

encantador/a (*adj*) wonderful, great, charming [18]

encantar (v) to captivate or charm (*Me encanta viajar = I love traveling; ¡Me encantó! = I loved it!*) [1, 4, 16, 19, 20]

un encanto de persona a wonderful person [1]

enchufado/a (*n*) [col, Spain] someone who got hired because of a contact [11]

en forma fit, in shape (*ponerse en forma = to get fit*) [14]

enfriar (v) to get cold [5]

engañar (a alguien) (v) to deceive or trick (someone) [12]

engordar (v) to get fatter, to gain weight [14]

enrollarse (con alguien) (v) [col, Spain] to get involved (with someone) [2]

en todo caso anyway, in any event [7]

entrar (v) bien/de maravilla [Spain] to go down well/really well (*for a drink*) [7]

entrar hambre/sed/sueño [Spain] *See Me está entrando hambre* [19]

(no) entrar (v) en la ropa [Spain] (not) to fit into one's clothes [14]

envidioso/a (*adj and n*) envious [18]

Era un decir Don't take it the wrong way (*literally, it was just a saying*) [3]

escaparate (*nm*) shop window, window display [8]

escupir (v) to spit (out) [7]

Es la época It's that time of year [17]

Es la monda [col, Spain] He/She/It's a real blast; He/She/It's really funny [4, 9]

Es lo de menos That's the least of it; That doesn't matter [11]

Eso es asunto mío That's my business [10]

espanto (*nm*) *See ¡Qué espanto!* [4]

Está bien All right, OK [12]

Estamos en paz We're quits; We're even [12]

estar a tope [col, Spain] to be very busy [11]

estar como una foca to be really fat [14, 15]

estar hasta el gorro [Spain] to have had it, to be fed up (*See "Letting off Steam" in Unit 11 for other similar expressions.*) [11]

estar hecho/a una pena [Spain] to be a wreck, a sorry sight [17]

estar hecho/a polvo [col] to be a wreck (*physically or emotionally*) [21]

estar loco/a por (alguien) to be crazy about (someone) [1]

estar mal de dinero to be broke or hard up for money [10]

estar quedado/a (con alguien) [col, Spain] to be hung up on someone [1]

estar sin un duro [col, Spain] to be broke (*See "Pleading Poverty" in Unit 10 for other expressions.*) [10]

Esto es vida This is the life [20]

Estoy dudando entre A y B I can't make up my mind between *A* and *B* [15]

Estoy en ello I'm working on it [15]

estupendo/a (*adj*) great, fantastic [4]

etiqueta (*nf*) price tag [8]

excursión (*nf*) a day trip, an excursion [13]

explotado/a (*adj*) developed, built up [13]

exterior (*adj*) [Spain] outward-facing (*opening onto the street*) [16]

extravagante (*adj*) outlandish, flamboyant [18]

F

factura (*nf*) bill, invoice [10]

falso/a (*adj*) phony, fake [3]

fatal (*adj*) terrible (*more common in Spain than in Latin America*) [3, 17]

favorecer (*v*) to suit [6]

fenomenal (*adj*) [col, Spain] great [4]

Fíjate Just think!, Get this!; Just look at . . . , Get a load of . . . [2, 17, 18]

finca (*nf*) ranch, estate [19]

forrado/a [Spain] loaded, rolling in it (*used in some Latin American countries, e.g., Chile*) [10]

forrarse (*v*) [Spain] to get rich [10]

fresco/a brazen or cheeky [5]

fresquito/a (*adj, dim*) cool, chilly [5]

friolero/a (*adj and n*) cold-blooded ([LA] *friolento/a*) [5]

fuera del presupuesto not in my budget, beyond my budget [16]

fuerte (*adj*) [col] shocking, disturbing [4]

fuertote (*adj*) robust, strong (*from fuerte, "strong"*) [14]

G

gafas de sol [Spain] sunglasses ([LA] *lentes de sol*) [20]

ganar (*v*) to earn or win [10]

ganar (*v*) **peso** to gain weight [14]

ganga (*nf*) bargain [12]

gastos (*n, pl*) expenses [10]

gazpacho (*nm*) a cold tomato-based soup (*a typical summer dish in Spain*) [5, 15]

genial (*adj*) [col] great, wonderful [1, 4, 9, 18]

goloso/a (*adj and n*) sweet-toothed (*ser goloso/a = to have a sweet tooth*) [15]

una gozada (*nf*) [Spain] great, wonderful, a real treat ([syn] *una delicia*) [14]

gracioso/a (*adj*) funny, witty [4, 13, 18, 21] cute, attractive [6]

grasa (*nf*) fat [14]

grave (*adj*) serious [17]

gringo/a (*n*) [LA] American or foreigner of Anglo-Saxon descent (*a little pejorative*) [13]

gripe (*nf*) flu ([var] *un gripazo*) [17]

guaperas (*nm*) [Spain] a stud, a good-looking suave guy (*negative*) [1]

guapo/a (*adj*) beautiful, handsome (*also used to address friends*) [1, 3, 6, 17]

guiri (*n*) [col, Spain] a foreigner (*generally white and from a non-Latin culture; a little pejorative*) [9, 21]

gustar (*v*) to please, to be pleasing (*Me gusta ese escritor = I like that writer, but me gustas = I "fancy" you*) [1, 9, 14, 15, 16, 20]

H

hace falta one needs, we need [18]

hacer la compra to do the shopping, to buy groceries [8]

hacer la pelota [Spain] to brownnose or try to ingratiate oneself [11] hacer la ruta (maya, románica, del vino...) to do the (Mayan, Romanesque, wine . . .) route [13]

hacer pesas to lift weights [14]

hacer vida sana to live healthily [14]

Haces bien Good idea; You're right (*to do something*) [15]

Hace un sol de justicia [Spain] The sun's really strong [20]

¡Hala! Whoa! My goodness! [19]

helado/a (*adj*) frozen, freezing [5]

hijo/a [Spain] kiddo [13, 17, 21]

historia (*nf*) [col, Spain] a relationship or affair [1]

las horas de luz the daylight hours [13]

horroroso/a (*adj*) dreadful, awful [4]; ugly, hideous [6]

hortera (*adj* and *n*) [Spain] tacky, bad taste [18]

un huevo [col] a lot (*vulgar*) [8]

I

ideal (*adj*) beautiful, perfect, great, wonderful [6]

un/a imbécil (*n*) a jerk or idiot [3]

inaguantable (*adj*) unbearable, intolerable [3]

ingresar (*v*) [Spain] to deposit (into a bank account) ([LA] *depositar*) [10]

insoportable (*adj*) unbearable, very annoying or tedious [3, 4, 11]

interesado/a (*adj* and *n*) self-seeking, out for himself/herself [18]

interior (*adj*) [Spain] inward-facing (*facing onto an inner courtyard*) [16]

ir a medias [Spain] to go fifty-fifty, to go Dutch [10]

ir de (rico, diva...) to act like one's (rich, a prima donna, etc.) [10, 18]

ir de compras to go shopping [8]

ir de tiendas [Spain] to go shopping [8]

J

jarabe (*nm*) syrup [17]

jarra (*nf*) pitcher, jug [7]

jefe/jefa (*n*) boss [11]

juerga (*nf*) blast, blow out, good time (*estar/ir de juerga* = *to be/go out partying and having a good time; see "Out on the Town" in Unit 9*) [9]

justo/a (*adj*) tight ([var] *justito/a*) [8]

L

lagarto (*nm*) sun-worshipper (*literally, lizard*) [20]

levantar (*v*) la moral to raise one's spirits [2]

ligar (a alguien) (*v*) [col, Spain] (*loosely translated*) to pick up or score (*See "Getting Together" in Unit 2.*) [2]

ligero/a (*adj*) light [15]

ligue (*nm*) [col, Spain] a casual fling or relationship; a person with whom one is having a casual fling [2]

lío (*nm*) [col, Spain] an affair or fling (*more generally, un lío is a messy or confusing situation*) [1]

listo/a (*adj* and *n*) clever, smart [18]

llamativo/a (*adj*) flashy, attention-getting [6]

Llena mucho It's really filling [15]

llevar (un mes) juntos to have been together (for a month) [2]

llevarse (*v*) to take or buy [8, 12]

llevarse (bien/mal) (*v*) to get along (well/badly) [2, 11]

Lo que oyes [col] Seriously; I'm not kidding [19]

lucir (*v*) to show off, to parade, to display [20]

luminoso/a (*adj*) bright, with lots of light [16]

M

machacar (*v*) [col] to wear down, to put through the grinder (*literally, to crush or to grind*) [21]

madrugada (*nf*) early morning, dawn, daybreak (*madrugar* = *to get up early*) [21]

majo/a (*adj*) [Spain] nice [18]

una marca (*nf*) a brand (*de marca* = *a brand name, a designer label*) [8]

marcha (*n*) [col, Spain] energy, particularly for partying (*See "Out on the Town" in Unit 9.*) [9]

marea (*nf*) tide (*marea alta/baja* = *high/low tide*) [20]

marearse (*v*) to feel faint, to get dizzy [17]

un marroquí/italiano/mejicano (*nm*) [Spain] a Moroccan/Italian/Mexican restaurant [6]

matorral (*nm*) brush, thicket, scrub [19]

me apetece I feel like; I'm in the mood for ([LA] *se me antoja*) [15]

me cae bien I like (him/her) ([var] *me cae genial* = *I really like (him/her)*) [1, 18]

me cae mal/fatal I dislike/really dislike (him/her) [3]

Me da igual It doesn't matter, I don't care [15]

¡Me da un ataque! I'd die! I'd have a heart attack! (*Casi me da un ataque* = *It almost gave me a heart attack*) [10, 20]

Me da (un) mal rollo [col, Spain] It really turns me off; It's a turn-off [15]

un/a médico de cabecera (*n*) a general practitioner, a family doctor [17]

Me duele (la rodilla) (My knee) hurts [17]

Me está entrando hambre/sed/sueño [Spain] I'm getting hungry/thirsty/sleepy ([LA] *Me está dando hambre, etc.*) [19]

Me hace gracia I find him/her/it amusing or appealing [18]

Menos mal Thank God! [5, 13]

el menú del día lunch special, prix fixe lunch [15]

me pone enfermo/a [Spain] (He/She/It) makes me sick ([LA] *Me enferma*) [3]

me pone malo/a [Spain] (He/She/It) makes me sick ([LA] *Me enferma*) [3]

Me reservo (*v*) **para (el postre)** I'm saving room for (dessert) [15]

meterse (*v*) **con (algo/alguien)** to verbally attack or criticize (something/someone) [3]

meterse (*v*) **en (un sitio, el agua, la cama)** to go or get into (a place, the water, bed) [14, 20, 21]

michelines (*nm, pl*) [Spain] love handles ([LA] *los rollos*) [14]

mochila (*nf*) backpack [19]

la monda [col, Spain] really funny, a real blast [4, 9]

mono/a (*adj*) [Spain] cute, pretty ([var] *una monada* [6])

montar (un negocio) (*v*) [Spain] to set up (one's own business) ([syn] *poner un negocio*) [11, 19]

el monte the mountains [19]

un montón (de gente) [col] a lot (of people) [14]

morirse del asco [col, Spain] to not be able to take (something) [19]

moverse (*v*) to get around [13]

muermo/a (*n*) [col, Spain] boring, someone/something lacking in zest or energy [9]

N

negarse (a hacer algo) (*v*) to refuse (to do something) [17]

¡Ni loco/a! No way! I'd have to be crazy! [16]

¡Ni muerto/a! No way! Not even if I were dead! [16]

¡Ni que lo digas! [Spain] You said it; I'll second that [11]

No cuelgues Hold on (*for the telephone*) [17]

no dar ni golpe to do nothing, to be idle [11]

No doy más abasto I can't cope; It's more than I can handle [21]

No hay ni un alma There isn't a soul; It's totally deserted [13]

no llevar nada encima [Spain] to not have any money on one [10]

¡No me digas! No!, You're joking! [1, 19]

No me extraña No wonder; It doesn't surprise me [8]

No me fío I don't trust (*you, it, him, her, etc.*) [15]

No me va [col, Spain] He/She isn't my type; It's not my style [2]

no parar to be really busy (*literally, to not stop*) [11]

No pasa nada It's no big deal; Don't worry [8, 14]

no pegar ojo to not sleep a wink [21]

No puedo más I've had it [11]

No puedo más con... I can't take . . . ; I can't deal or cope with . . . [5]

Normal [Spain] Of course, Naturally [18]

No suena mal It doesn't sound bad [16]

No tengo más remedio I have no choice; I've got no other option [16]

novio/a (*n*) boy/girlfriend (*can also be fiancé/e*) [2, 9, 10, 18]

O

un/a obseso/a (del jazz) a (jazz) nut [15]

odiar (*v*) to hate [3, 20]

odioso/a (*adj*) creepy, despicable [3]

¡Oiga! Excuse me! (*used to get someone's attention, e.g., waiters*) [9]

un ojo de la cara an arm and a leg, a fortune [3]

ola (*nf*) wave [20]

¡Olvídate! [col] Forget it! No way! [20]

ordenador (*nm*) [Spain] computer ([LA] *computadora*) [11]

organizarse (*v*) to get one's act together [11]

original (*adj*) original, inventive, fun [4, 6]

P

pachucho/a (*adj*) [Spain] under the weather, not feeling great [17]

pagar cada uno lo suyo to pay one's share [10]

¡Para ya! [Spain] Stop it! That's enough! [5]

¡Pareces otro/a! Wow, you look great! [6]

paro (*nm*) [Spain] unemployment (*vivir del paro* = *to live off unemployment benefits*) [11]

pasado/a de moda outdated, passé [4]

pasarse (*v*) to push it, to go too far, to overdo it, to go overboard [9, 15]

Paso de (algo/alguien) [col, Spain] I have no interest in (something/someone) [4]

pasta (*nf*) [col, Spain] money (*una pasta* = *a fortune, a lot of money*) ([LA] *plata*) [10]

pastel (*nm*) cake [15]

pastilla (*nf*) pill, tablet [17]

patatas bravas (*nf, pl*) fried potatoes in a spicy tomato sauce (*a typical* **tapa** *in Madrid*) [9]

pedir (*v*) to order (*in a bar or restaurant*), to ask for [9, 12, 15, 20]

pedo (*adj and n*) [col, Spain] smashed, wasted, drunk [7]

pegado/a (a la tele) glued (to the TV) [11]

Pega fuerte It's really hot; The sun's beating down hard [20]

pegar saltos to jump up and down [14]

pegarse un baño [Spain] to take a dip [20]

peli (*nf*) [col, Spain] movie, film (*abbreviated form of* película) [4]

un pelín (*adv*) [col, Spain] a little [9]

pelma (*n and adj*) [col, Spain] a pain in the neck, a bore [5]

pendiente (*nf*) slope, incline (*Tiene mucha pendiente* = *It's very steep*) [19]

el/la penúltimo/a one for the road, the last round (*literally, the second to last*) [9]

perder la cabeza (por alguien) (*v*) to fall madly in love (with someone) [1]

perdido/a (*adv*) [col, Spain] totally (*tonto perdido* = *totally stupid*) [1, 7]

pesadilla (*nf*) nightmare [21]

pesado/a (*n*) a bore, a pain in the neck; (*adj*) boring, tedious; heavy, rich (*for food*) [1, 3, 5, 15, 19, 21]

pescado (*nm*) fish (*as food*) [14]

petardo/a (*n*) [col, Spain] a bore or pain in the ass [3, 7]

pez (*nm*) fish (*the live animal*) [20]

pez gordo big shot, VIP (*literally, fat fish*) [11]

pibe/piba (*n*) [LA] boy/girl (*common in Argentina; used by some young people in Spain*) [2]

picar (*v*) to nibble or snack on [9]

pillar (*v*) [col] to get [5]

pirarse (*v*) [col, Spain] to beat it, to split, to leave quickly [12]

piso (*nm*) floor, story; [Spain] an apartment with two or more bedrooms [16]

plato (*nm*) dish; course [15]

playero/a (*adj*) beach (*from* una playa, *a beach*) [20]

poner (*v*) [Spain] to serve (*for food and drink*) [9]

poner a parir (a alguien) [col, Spain] to diss or speak badly of (someone) [3]

poner mala cara to pout, grimace, or give a dirty look [8]

ponerse las pilas [col] to get moving, to get on the job [16]

ponerse morado/a [col, Spain] to pig out [15]

por cierto by the way [6, 14, 19, 20, 21]

Por intentarlo no pierdes nada You've got nothing to lose by trying [12]

por lo visto (*adv*) apparently [18]

postre (*nm*) dessert [15]

practicar deportes to do sports [19]

precioso/a (*adj*) beautiful, gorgeous ([var] *una preciosidad*) [6]

prenda (*nf*) item of clothing [8]

preparado/a (*adj*) competent, able [18]

presentar a alguien (*v*) to introduce someone (*to somebody*) [2]

prestar (*v*) to lend [10]

previsor/a (*adj*) sensible, prudent [10]

probador (*nm*) changing room [8] (*Not used in all Latin American countries*)

probar (*v*) to try or taste (*for food and drink*); to try on (*for clothes*) [7, 8, 9]

profe (*n*) [col, Spain] teacher (*abbreviated form of profesor/a*) [7]

progre (*adj*) liberal [18]

protagonista (*n*) hero/heroine, main character [4]

pub (*nm*) a nightclub or bar [9]

puesto (*nm*) stall [12]

Q

¡Qué asco! Gross! How disgusting! [4]

quedar (*v*) to stay; to remain or be left, to be (*for fit or location*); to look, to buy or take (*See "A Catch-All Verb" in Unit 8 for explanations and examples.*) [6, 8, 10, 12, 13, 16, 19, 20, 21]

quedar (con alguien) (*v*) [Spain] to have a plan to get together (with someone) (*See "Getting Together" in Unit 2.*) [2, 6, 9]

quedarse (*v*) **frito/a** [col] to be out like a light, to fall asleep, to nod off [21]

¡Qué dices! [Spain] Are you kidding! [5, 8, 16, 17, 18]

¡Qué envidia! I'm so jealous! That sounds great! [6, 13]

¡Qué espanto! Dreadful! How appalling! (*¡Qué espanto de libro!* = *What a dreadful book!*) [4]

¡Qué horror! Awful! How awful! (*¡Qué horror de película!* = *What an awful movie!*) [4]

¡Qué maravilla! Wonderful! Amazing! [4, 13]

¡Qué pasada! [col, Spain] Wow! That's amazing! [13]

quemado/a (*adj*) [Spain] burned out [11]

quemarse (*v*) to get burned [20]

¿Qué más da? So what? Who cares? [19]

que no veas [col, Spain] like you wouldn't believe, a lot [17]

¿Qué pasa? [col, Spain] What's up? What do you mean? [6, 9, 21]

¡Qué peligro! [col, Spain] Uh oh! Oh dear! [1, 15]

¡Qué suerte! Lucky you! [2]

querer (*v*) to love; to want [1]

¿Qué tal te cayó? What did you think of him/her? Did you like him/her? [2]

que te mueres [col] great, fantastic, to die for [9]

¿Qué te pareció (la película, etc.**)** What did you think of (the movie, *etc.*)? [4, 20]

¡Qué va! Ha! On the contrary! [11]

el quinto pino [Spain] very far away, out in the boondocks [16]

quitarse (el pan) (*v*) [Spain] to cut out, to stop having (bread) [14]

R

racha (*nf*) period, stretch of time ([Spain] *Llevo una racha que no paro* = *I've been really busy lately*) [11]

ración (*nf*) [Spain] large snack or serving [9]

raro/a (*adj*) strange, weird [18]

el Rastro (*nm*) the outdoor flea market in Madrid [12]

rebajado/a (*adj*) marked down, on sale [8]

las rebajas (*n, pl*) the sales (*las ofertas* in Mexico, *las liquidaciones* in Chile and Argentina) [6, 10]

recetar (*v*) to prescribe [17]

recorrer (*v*) to tour, to travel around [13]

reformado/a (*adj*) renovated [16]

refrescar (*v*) to refresh, to cool down [20]

refresco (*nm*) soft drink [20]

regatear (*v*) to bargain or haggle (*el regateo* = *bargaining, haggling*) [12]

régimen (*nm*) [Spain] diet ([syn] *dieta*) [14, 15]

relación (*nf*) relationship [2]

la relación calidad-precio value for the money (*buena relación calidad-precio* = *good value, very reasonable*) [8]

rentable (*adj*) profitable [11]

repelente (*adj*) disgusting, repulsive [4]

repugnante (*adj*) horrible, disgusting [3]

resaca (*nf*) hangover (*not used in all Latin American countries*) [7]

reserva (*nm*) special vintage (*for wine*) [7]

un resfriado (*nm*) a cold [5, 17]

retirado/a (*adj*) off the beaten track [19]

revelar (*v*) to develop (*photographs, film*) [13]

rico/a (*adj*) rich, wealthy; delicious, good (*for food and drink*) [7, 10, 15]

un robo [col] a rip-off, too expensive [12]

un rollo [col, Spain] a pain or drag [13]

romper (con alguien) (*v*) to break up (with someone) [1]

ronda (*v*) round (*of drinks*) [9]

roto/a (*adj*) [col, Spain] exhausted, beat [21]

S

sacar de quicio to irritate or get on one's nerves [3]

Sales como nuevo/a You come out feeling new [14]

salir (con alguien) (*v*) to go out with someone [2]

salir (del agua) (*v*) to get out (of the water) [20]

sano/a (*adj*) healthy, wholesome ([var] *sanote/a* = *robust, healthy*) [2, 11, 14]

seguir (con alguien) (*v*) to still be seeing/going out (with someone) [2]

sendero (*nm*) path, trail [19]

ser de constitución (delgada/fuerte) to have a (small/large) frame or build [14]

¿Se te ha pasado...? Have you gotten over . . . ? [17]

Se (te) nota (*v*) It shows; You can tell [14]

Se trata de... It's about . . . ; You're supposed to . . . [7]

Se van a enterar [col, Spain] They're gonna get it; They've got it coming [12]

sibarita (*adj* and *n*) gourmet, epicurean [15]

la sierra the mountains [19]

siesta (*nf*) a post-lunch nap [21]

simpático/a (*adj*) friendly, nice [18]

un/a sinvergüenza (*n*) a shameless person, someone with nerve [10]

sitios de ligar [col, Spain] singles' bars [2]

Sobre gustos no hay nada escrito There's no accounting for tastes [18]

socorrista (*n*) lifeguard [20]

soñar (con alguien/algo) (*v*) to dream (about someone/something) [21]

sonarse (la nariz) (*v*) to blow one's nose [17]

soportar (*v*) to tolerate or stand (*No la soporto* = *I can't stand her*) [3]

sorbito (*nm, dim*) sip [7]

sudar (*v*) to sweat [14]

sueldo (*nm*) salary [10]

sueño (*nm*) dream, sleepiness (*tener sueño* = *to be sleepy; tener un sueño* = *to have a dream*) [21]

sumamente (*adv*) totally, completely [4]

super (*adv*) [col] really, very [6, 18]

el surf (*n*) surfing (*un/a surfista* = *a surfer*) [20]

T

tacaño/a (*n*) cheapskate, miser; (*adj*) stingy, tight-fisted [10]

talla (*nf*) size [8]

las tantas the wee hours, very late at night or very early in the morning [21]

tapa (*nf*) [Spain] small snack, usually served before meals [9]

Tarda (una hora) It takes (an hour) [19]

tema (*nm*) [col, Spain] things, the "thing" [18]

temporada alta/baja high/low season [13]

tener buen tipo [Spain] to have a good figure [6]

tener buena pinta to look good [15]

tener ganas de (hacer algo) to feel like (doing something), to really want (to do something), to be eager (to do something) (*See "¡Ojo!" in Unit 21 for examples.*) [21]

tener (mal) genio to have a (bad) temper [18]

tener mala leche [col, Spain] to be nasty or vindictive [18]

tener manía (a alguien) [Spain] to dislike (someone) [18]

tener marcha [col, Spain] to be full of energy, to be into the nightlife or "action" (*See "Out on the Town" in Unit 9.*) [9]

tensión (*nf*) blood pressure ([LA] *la presión*) [17]

terraza (*nf*) [Spain] an outdoor café [5]

timo (*nm*) a rip-off [8]

tinto (*nm* and *adj*) red (wine) [7]

tío/a (*n*) [col, Spain] guy or gal (*also used informally to address friends and acquaintances*) [1, 2, 3, 4, 5, 10, 12, 14, 16, 17, 18, 19]

tipo (*nm*) type; figure, body ([var] *un tipito* = *a good figure*) [2, 6, 14]

tirado/a (*adj*) [col, Spain] a steal, really cheap ([syn] *regalado/a*) [12]

tirar (*v*) to pull (*in this case, "pull" draft beer*) [9]

tirar (*v*) **el dinero** to throw money out the window [10]

títulos de crédito [Spain] credits ([LA] *los créditos*) [4]

tomar (*v*) to have (*for food and drink*) [5, 7, 9, 15, 19]

tomar (*v*) **algo por ahí** to go out for a drink and/or snack [9]

tomar (*v*) **el sol** to sunbathe, to sit or lie in the sun [20]

un toro bravo a fighting bull (*a bull bred for bullfighting*) [19]

tos (*nf*) cough, coughing [17]

Total Anyway; To sum things up [11]

trago (*nm*) gulp (*tragar* = *to swallow*) [7]

tragón/tragona (*n*) big eater, glutton [15]

Tranquilo/a Calm down; Don't worry [3, 8, 16]

trasladarse (de casa) (*v*) [Spain] to move (house) ([syn] *mudarse*) [16]

tremendo/a (*adj*) big, colossal; [col, Spain] outrageous, extreme [4, 13, 17, 18]

tripa (*nf*) [Spain] belly [14]

triunfar (*v*) to make it, to be very successful [11]

tumbarse (*v*) to lie down [21]

U

urgencias (*nf, pl*) the emergency room [17]

V

Va en serio It's serious; It's for real [2]

última oferta last offer [12]

unas vacaciones (*nf, pl*) a vacation [11, 13]

las vacas locas mad cows, mad cow disease [15]

vale [col, Spain] OK, all right [1, 8, 9, 16]

Vale mucho He/She has really wonderful qualities; He's/She's really talented [18]

valer (*v*) **para algo** to be good at something [12]

vaqueros (*nm, pl*) [Spain] jeans ([LA] *jeans*) [8]

vaso (*nm*) glass (*for water and nonalcoholic beverages*) [7]

Vaya Ah-ha; Oh dear [4, 10, 11, 16, 21]

vecino/a (*n*) neighbor [16]

vendedor/a (*n*) vendor, seller [12]

Venga [col, Spain] Come on; OK; Good idea [3, 4, 5, 7, 8, 9, 10, 12, 15, 16, 18, 19, 21]

Venga, va [col, Spain] OK, you're on [4]

¡Venga ya! [col, Spain] Oh come on! Oh please! [5, 19]

veraneante (*n*) summer vacationer [20]

ver los monumentos to see the sights, to go sightseeing [13]

verdurita (*nf, dim*) veggies [14]

¡Vete tú a saber! God knows! Your guess is as good as mine! [9]

un viaje organizado a package tour [13]

víbora (*nf*) person with a vicious tongue (*literally, a viper*) [18]

virgen (*adj*) unspoiled, natural, wild [13]

visitar la ciudad to visit a city, to go sightseeing [13]

vital (*adj*) high-energy, full of life [18]

vuelo (*nm*) flight [13]

Y

Ya [Spain] Yes, I know [10]

Ya es hora It's about time [2]

¡Ya está bien! That's enough! [5]

Ya te digo [col, Spain] You said it; You're telling me [19]

Y ni te cuento lo de… And I won't even go into . . . [10]

y no hay tu tía [Spain] And that's that; And there's no getting around it [17]

¿Y qué? So what? [20]

¿Y (tu novio) qué? What about (your boyfriend)? [9]

Z

zona (*nf*) area [13, 16]

9 780071 415149